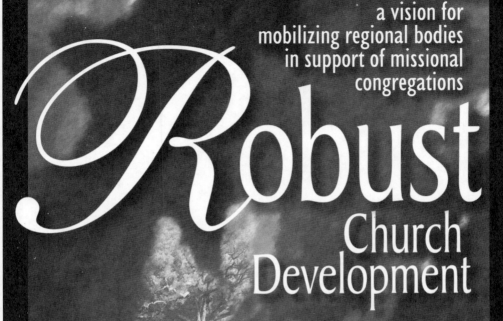

a vision for
mobilizing regional bodies
in support of missional
congregations

$\mathscr{R}$obust
Church
Development

Mike Regele

Data presented in Chapters 4 and 5 are drawn from Percept's Survey of Congregational Development in U.S. Denominations, conducted in the fall of 2001. For further information about this research refer to Percept's website at www.percept.info, as well as the various reports of finding available to download.

For additional printed copies, contact Percept at (800) 442-6277, or go to www.percept.info and order online.

Cover design and illustrations by Tom Hoyt

Printed in the United States of America on Recycled Paper

00 01 02 03 - 10 9 8 7 6 5 4 3 2 1

About the Author

MIKE REGELE (M. Div.) studied at Seattle Pacific University and Fuller Theological Seminary. He is co-founder and president of Percept, and an author and co-author whose published works include, *Death of the Church (Harper Collins/Zondervan, 1995)*, *Exploring Your Ministry Area*, *Your Church and Its Mission*, *Understanding Your Congregation*, *ReVision* and *Crossing the Bridge: Church Leadership in a Time of Change (Percept, 2000)*.

PERCEPT, since its inception in 1988, has supplied thousands of churches and parishes, and hundreds of regional and national denominational agencies with demographic resources to help them engage in mission within their particular context. Percept adds value to its demographic information by integrating data about the religious attitudes, preferences and behavior of the American people. Percept has regularly been recognized as one of the best strategic information companies in the country.

Acknowledgments

For those who write, there is always a keen awareness that such projects are derived from many sources. This book is no different. Some contributed ideas. Some contributed information. Some contributed stories. And some contributed support. As the writer, the task is to weave these strands into a picture of a proposed reality. It is only fitting that those contributions be recognized.

First of all, I wish to thank my mother, Geneva Regele and my son, Jonathan for their faith stories. Together, they inspired me in the definition of one of the key elements of this vision.

I would also like to thank the many denominational clients who participated in the Congregational Development Survey Percept fielded in the Fall of 2001. Their responses and the picture portrayed in the aggregate became the driving force of this entire project.

My colleagues within Percept are always a source of great inspiration and at times, an important critical sounding board. Many ideas presented here were first floated in casual conversations or early written drafts. The final form reflects the important input each of them gave. I wish to thank each one of them for their wisdom and professional expertise. The ideas have more depth and grounding in real life because of them.

Finally, I am most grateful to my family. For my dear wife Debra for her years of support and encouragement. And for my children, Jonathan, Justin, Jordan, Kiersten and Ellissa whose lives have given such richness and hope to my own.

Contents

Foreward

"Ideas matter!" Though I cannot remember where I heard this, the notion has stayed with me for years. Ideas matter because they give expression to creativity. And through creative ideas, we create our worlds. One could say, therefore, that ideas drive action. We need strong action in support of congregations today, but strong action must be driven by creative ideas. This is the role vision plays in the life of any endeavor or organization. Without creative ideas, action becomes simply a reaction to someone else's ideas.

This book reflects a proactive attempt by Percept to set forth an idea. That idea revolves around our hopes and dreams for our regional body clients' congregational or church development efforts. For 15 years we have been working in partnership with regional and national denominational agencies to support the development of vital congregations. Percept is now looking forward to our next 5 years of partnership. In the process, we have asked ourselves: What would the development efforts of our clients look like if they were effective in their work of assisting congregations? And based upon that vision, what role can and should we play as partners, assisting where we can to help them get there?

Before proceeding any further, we want to address a potential terminology problem. In our early years, our primary clients were regional bodies of the Presbyterian Church (USA), The Episcopal Church, the United Methodist Church and the Evangelical Lutheran Church in America. These traditions refer to the task of assisting congregations start or respond to their changing environment as "congregational development." However, in recent years, our client family has broadened significantly, now encompassing other Protestant groups as well as Roman

Catholic Archdioceses and Dioceses. The terminology of congregational development is not often used in these traditions and we have found at times a need to translate. Almost all traditions seem to understand the term of "church development" as encompassing those activities we often associated with congregational development. So, in order to make this book as broadly readable as possible, we are adopting the term "church development" except in those cases where "congregational development" is required for historical or documentary reasons. For the purposes of this book, the two terms are interchangeable.

In this book, we set forth a vision for a robust church development effort. The book is one of many pieces that together will comprise our efforts to support and resource the efforts of those on the frontline of engagement with congregations. It has its origin in a research project conducted in the fall of 2001 and through much of 2002. Consequently, much of the idea is derived from listening to our clients. The ideas were first shaped and conveyed publicly during Percept's 2003 client conference in San Diego, CA. For those who attended that event, you will recognize much of the material presented here, though it has been reshaped to fit a book format.

Over the next five years, Percept will focus on assisting its clients to develop robust church development efforts. The role of this book is to present the idea, or, if you will, the vision. While the ideas are outlined here, the book is only a beginning, one element of a multi-faceted strategy that we will unfold between now and 2007. Over the next five years, you can look forward to some of the following.

1. *Two client conferences will be conducted, one in the winter of 2005 and one in the winter of 2007. The focus of each conference will be on progress toward robust efforts. Each will build upon the ideas laid down in 2003. We look forward to identifying regional bodies who are seeing the robust vision realized. Having identified these bodies, some of them will be invited to share with the rest of us. Our hope is that 2007 will be a celebration of transformation and robustness.*

2. *New leadership resources will be rolled out that support you in developing your robust effort. Already we have several assessment tools that are available to our clients online. There are a few more on the "drawing board." While we cannot be too specific at this time, we can say that all leadership resources will support the 10 Best Practices you will find outlined in this book.*

3. *Planning models and processes in support of mission, both locally and regionally, have been part of Percept's offerings for years. Some existing programs will be updated and expanded. And we are looking to add some planning pieces that will assist in annual program evaluation, goal setting and budgeting—these will be directly tied to one of the Best Practices.*

4. *One important goal driving some resource development is to increase the leadership capacity to lead a robust effort. Toward that end, we are considering some different ways to partner with our clients and assist them to develop greater leadership capability. Again, we cannot be too specific at this time, but we are ready to extend our partnership in this direction around those concerns that are relevant to the kinds of tools and resources we provide.*

5. *And of course we will continue to provide our clients with the best, most usable community information while maintaining cost-effectiveness—the hallmark of our first 15 years.*

Ideas matter. They can reflect the expression of imaginative thought. Imagination takes form as ideas. We present to you this book as an idea. The idea is simple. We want to see regional denominational bodies develop a robust church development effort. What does this mean? What does it look like? That is the subject of this book. We present it to our client world, both those who are currently clients and those whom we hope will join us—as a framework within which to think and discuss how each of you thinks about and actualizes your efforts on behalf of congregations.

Percept believes God called us into existence to serve you in your journey of serving congregations. It is our prayer that this book provides one little bit of assistance along the way.

Respectfully on behalf of my two partners, Mark Schulz and Peter Wernett, and the entire Percept Team,

Mike Regele
May 2003

A Captivating Vision

Forty years ago, on the steps of the Lincoln Memorial in Washington, D.C., Reverend Dr. Martin Luther King, Jr., stood and delivered his famous "I Have a Dream" speech. It was a galvanizing moment in the battle for civil rights in America. He began with these words:

> Five score years ago, a great American, in whose symbolic shadow we stand signed the Emancipation Proclamation. This momentous decree came as a great beacon light of hope to millions of Negro slaves who had been seared in the flames of withering injustice. It came as a joyous daybreak to end the long night of captivity. But one hundred years later, we must face the tragic fact that the Negro is still not free.

He continued to describe the injustices that the African-American community faced one hundred years later, a situation that was intolerable and that needed to change. But change to what? He had a dream:

> I have a dream that one day this nation will rise up and live out the true meaning of its creed: "We hold these truths to be self-evident: that all men are created equal." I have a dream that one day on the red hills of Georgia the sons of former slaves and the sons of former slaveowners will be able to sit down together at a table of brotherhood. I have a dream that one day even the state of Mississippi, a desert state, sweltering with the heat of injustice and oppression, will be transformed into an oasis of freedom and justice. I have a dream that my four children will one day live in a nation where they will not be judged by the color of their skin but by the content of their character. I have a dream today.

He continued tying his particular dream to the biblical vision of redemption of the world:

> I have a dream that one day every valley shall be exalted, every hill

and mountain shall be made low, the rough places will be made plain, and the crooked places will be made straight, and the glory of the Lord shall be revealed, and all flesh shall see it together. This is our hope. This is the faith with which I return to the South. With this faith we will be able to hew out of the mountain of despair a stone of hope. With this faith we will be able to transform the jangling discords of our nation into a beautiful symphony of brotherhood. With this faith we will be able to work together, to pray together, to struggle together, to go to jail together, to stand up for freedom together, knowing that we will be free one day.

Dr. King had a dream. It was a large dream. It was a beautiful dream. It was a hope-filled dream. It was a dream that was founded upon and extended from his faith in God. As hard as it had been and would yet be, he refused to lose hope and that hope drove him forward. Our society today is very different—for the good—than it was 40 years ago. That is not to say we do not have a long way to go. But due to Dr. King's dream, a dream that drove him and thousands with him, America is a different society. Such is the power of great dreams.

The Power of a Dream

Dreams can be of two kinds. Some dreams are wishful thinking. Other dreams are captivating visions. Dreams that are simply wishful thinking seldom become more than thoughts that pass. Dreams, however, that are captivating visions capture the heart and imagination and compel one to act. They urge one on to see the dream transformed into reality in some way. Dr. King's dream was a captivating vision.

I have a dream as well. It is a dream that the churches across North America would be vital centers of life and hope. It is a dream that they would be places where people want to be. I dream of walking into any church in this country and feeling life and healing and acceptance. I dream of churches that know who they are and why they exist. I dream of churches that understand their calling from God and translate that calling into redemptive islands of hope for all people. I dream of churches that love their communities and lose themselves in the service of these communities. I dream of Christian churches wherein I can go and feel welcome and safe and accepted. I want this for myself. I want this for my children. I want this for others. It was the beauty of such a vision that made becoming a

Christian and joining the church so compelling to me over 30 years ago. This same dream continues to drive me today.

I wonder how many of you reading this share a similar dream? If you are reading this book, you most likely work in some way with local congregations. Surely you do so because in your heart you have a dream for these churches as well. Is your dream all that different from mine? I doubt it. Do you not want this for your churches, first, because you love them, and second, because you yourself want to have such an experience?

But is our dream really only wishful thinking? Or is our dream a captivating vision, compelling us forward to see it in some way made real? Is our dream driven by the kind of hope and faith that drove Dr. King? Or is it more like a Californian looking at the withering, dry hills wishing it would rain? The answer to this question will be quite clear based upon what we do. You are most likely involved in the support and service of local congregations from the perspective of a regional or national agency. That does not mean you are necessarily a denominational staff person. I suspect some readers are either pastors or lay-leaders who in addition to efforts at the local level, also serve through a regional structure.

But even more specifically, if you are reading this, you are most likely involved in what is generally labeled church development and usually incorporates working with or assisting congregations in the growth and development of their local ministries.

The question I want to pose to you is this: What will it take? What will it take to have our dream become more than wishful thinking? Can the efforts we call church development be a tool in transforming our dreams for our churches into reality? That is a good question. It is also the question we want to wrestle with in these pages. I would begin our quest toward answering it by stating that we must not only have a dream for our churches that captivates and compels us, we must also have a captivating vision for the work of church development itself.

Let me set the stage.

Setting the Stage

For the last 20 years, many of us working with churches and denominational agencies have been trying to sort out our changing social and cultural reality for the church in North America. The result has been fairly fruitful even if what we have come to understand is a bit disconcerting. Many of us are now comfortable with (or at least have resigned ourselves to) the notion of life in a postmodern world where the church has been displaced from the central role in our social and cultural life that it held for so long.

As a result, we are now in a continual discussion about how to redirect or transform congregations for this new North American context. If honest, we have greater clarity about what will not work than what will. But encouraging signs are emerging and some of the darkness that I sensed earlier in my career is giving way to a new hope and expectation—even though we recognize it will only come with a great deal of faith and work.

What is emerging is a model of the church that is displacing a Christendom Chaplaincy with that of the church as a missionary enterprise. The local congregation is now being reshaped as the frontline of mission. Our understanding of evangelism is evolving as well. For too long evangelism meant urging nominal Christians to take their cultural faith seriously and get back into the Christendom fold. Increasingly we are coming to grips with the notion that evangelism really means introducing people to the Christian faith and a relationship with God while inviting them into an alternative community.

What Is the Role of Regional and National Denominational Bodies?

While a new model for the local congregation, what the Diocese of Texas calls "mission stations" is taking root, there is less information available on the place and role of denominational bodies—both regional and national. The model for regional and national denominational agencies is just now beginning to be discussed in light of this new missionary reality. The question denominational agencies are now asking is this: What is our task if the local congregations have become mission stations?

Historically, whether regionally or nationally, agencies above the local congregation have served two primary functions:

1. *governance and regulation*
2. *resourcing and support of congregations*

Gil Rendle of the Alban Institute in a report titled, "Finding the Path in the Wilderness: Middle Judicatory Case Studies and Learnings" notes that these two roles "form a classic 'polarity'" that must be carefully managed.[1] Both are necessary. The first role generally revolves around setting and sustaining core theological traditions and the qualification of those leaders responsible to carry the tradition forward in local congregations. The second role is that of providing resources and support to local congregations. These twin historic roles remain, but in reality, many regional and national bodies are more skilled in the regulatory side of the polarity. And yet, with the changes occurring, the need of the local congregations for less regulation and greater resources and support has never been greater. Rendle notes, "The role of the middle judicatory office is now seen to be the first line of defense and the closest point of support for the important work and ministry of the local church."[2] He continues, "The role of the middle judicatory is to resource the local congregation—to help provide tools, insights, leadership training, or problem solutions needed to help the local congregation be effective in its own challenge of presenting and practicing faith in the specific immediacy of its own community."[3]

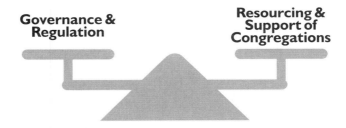

Bishop Claude Payne of the Diocese of Texas shares this view of the primary role of the regional agency. He says, "Because church growth is the result of congregational evangelism, the primary role of the judicatory should be to serve as a resource for the congregations.[4]

A New Vision for Denominational Bodies

For some years now, it has been "trendy" to say that we are entering a post-denominational era in the North American church. But I do not believe it needs to be this way. In fact, in our denominational systems and structures, we have a great untapped asset waiting to be put to work. We just need a new, captivating vision for these structures that will release and compel them in service of the churches. Our connectional systems, be they Episcopal structures or Baptist structures, are potentially well suited for the new role of supporting congregations on the frontline of mission. Part of the new vision is seeing a new role for our connectional structures and systems beyond the regulatory emphasis.

A new captivating vision would imagine and then shape the work of the regional governing bodies around a common hope of seeing vital congregations equipped to embrace their missionary challenge.

For many years now, those activities most focused on the local congregations—existing or to be planted—fell under various titles, such as Congregational Development or Church Development.[5] I must quickly point out that not all of our historic approaches will be effective under this revised vision. But the existing structures within our denominational organizations responsible for developing congregations is the most logical place for us to focus our efforts in developing support and resources for our churches.

I do not believe there is a more important task for regional or national level church bodies. While I will affirm Gil Rendle's dual function and believe both are necessary. I do not believe at the level of day to day functionality that the emphasis called for today is a balance between regulation and resourcing. We need to tilt the scales to the resourcing and support side. On a pessimistic note, if we do not focus extraordinary efforts on the health and vitality of our congregations that exist and those we need to start, there will be no need for the governance and regulatory function.

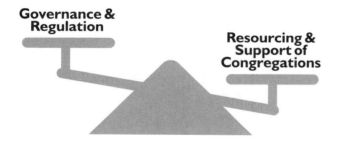

Governance & Regulation

Resourcing & Support of Congregations

On a more optimistic note, the missionary challenge before our churches today calls for a great effort. Assisting and encouraging local congregations to effectively engage their mission contexts is the great challenge and awesome possibility for regional church development today. Regional bodies must become the frontline of support for those on the frontline of mission in our culture.

A Robust Church Development Effort

What will it take to create regional bodies that can become this for their congregations? We contend that regional bodies will need to develop a robust effort in support of developing vital congregations. Or, to put it more directly, I believe all denominations in North America must of a first-order priority, commit themselves to a robust church development effort within their regional bodies. This will require more than simply stating that we will start new congregations, enhance the vitality of stable congregations and revitalize congregations experiencing struggles. A robust effort is more than this.

Quite frankly, this is my dream as well. While my ultimate dream is for vital congregations, I see the regional and national agencies of our denominational systems as critical to the renewal and revitalization of the churches in North America. This hope and vision drives Percept every day in working with our regional clients. We want to see each and every regional client evidencing a robust church development effort. This is why Mark Schulz and I started Percept in 1987, and why in 1990 Peter Wernett transplanted himself from the East Coast to the West to join two young, idealistic Boomers in their fledgling effort. We believe that if this vision is realized, the larger hope of vital and engaged congregations is more likely to become a reality.

In this book, we want to unpack this vision. Much of the content was first delivered to Percept's 2003 VISTA Client Conference in San Diego, CA. The reception of these ideas was very strong and positive. Therefore, we decided that these concepts needed to be translated into a small book that could be read across our entire client family, which in 2003 exceeds 300 regional- or national-level clients.

Part I will look at the shape of the vision. What does a robust church development effort look like? The first five chapters will focus on this question. Part II will explore how our regional bodies can become this vision of robustness. It is one thing to outline a full-bodied vision. It is quite another to translate that vision into reality in your home setting. Each of our clients comes from a different place, a different tradition and a different set of organizational issues and challenges. There is no simple formula that you can read and implement. The first two chapters of Part II will focus on the question of realizing the vision of a robust church development effort in your regional setting. Finally, having looked at the shape of the vision and ways to realize the vision, we must make a commitment personally to embrace the vision. What will the vision require of you? The last chapter will conclude on this theme.

A Robust Effort

What do I mean by a robust effort? Let's take this in two pieces. First, why "robust"? And second, what are the elements of such an effort?

What is the meaning of robust? Someone asked me why I chose this adjective to qualify "effort"? Why not a "successful," or "effective," or "efficient" or even "powerful" effort? Robust is such an odd word. Odd, yes, but you will remember it! Even more than its memorable value, the connotation of robust is exactly on target for what we need. If we have a robust effort, we have an effort that will meet the kind of challenge we face today—a challenge that is greater and calls for more than simply an efficient or successful effort.

Robust Design

The core meaning of robust is strong, like an oak. In Oregon, where I grew up as a kid, we had groves of large, gnarly oak trees. They were tough and withstood windstorms, ice storms and great heat. They were hearty, full-bodied trees. They were robust. Some of us define our coffee based upon the degree of its "robustness."

Robust connotes that which flourishes or that which prospers regardless of what swirls around it. The opposite of robustness is weakness and that which languishes—what fades away under duress. A weak effort may consume a great deal of time, but accomplishes little. A robust effort accomplishes much regardless of the challenges thrown at it.

There is a whole approach to engineering that is called "robust design." It has applications in design problems ranging from aircraft engineering to software development. I will not bore you with the particulars but the core idea is profound. A robust design will meet two objectives:

1. *It will create the capacity to minimize the impact of uncertainty on the mission or effort.*

2. *It will create maximum flexibility for responding to the changing environment.*

If these objectives are met, one is likely to have created a robust design that can deal with uncertainty without losing system stability.

The effect of robust design is a stable system that continues to function in the face of uncertainty and changing conditions. A robust design can withstand challenges thrown at it without losing its core capability—like an old oak tree in a nasty windstorm. In a rapidly changing environment, a system built upon a robust design is most likely to have the capacity to absorb variations and uncertainty and accomplish mission objectives.

Most of us would agree that the current situation facing most institutions in North America is rife with potential instability and uncertainty. Rigid organizational systems struggle to cope with the roller-coaster ride of modern life. Our churches face these kinds of challenges. Our regional and national denominational bodies do as well. To the extent that these systems do not reflect the objectives of a robust design, they are vulnerable to struggle, confusion and potentially failure.

When we think of our captivating vision for church development, we want it to reflect the characteristics of a robust design. We want our organizational systems to be shaped by the twin objectives of a robust design. Why? The changing context for the church in North America calls for denominational efforts that can deal with uncertainty that maximize flexibility while maintaining system stability. This is what we mean when we use the term "robust" to describe our vision for church development.

Now some questions for reflection: In all honesty, would you describe most of your church development efforts as meeting the objectives of a robust design? Can you identify points in your effort that do? Points that do not, and why?

Three Elements of a Robust Effort

We have looked at what we mean by a robust effort. Let us turn now to the second question: What are the elements of such an effort? If the task of regional level agencies is a robust effort in support of vital congregations, what are the elements of a robust church development effort? What does a robust church development effort look like?

I have thought about this long and hard since a phone conversation Peter Wernett and I had with Reverend Jim Powell, President of Church Extension for the Christian Church (Disciples of Christ). We were sharing with Jim some of the preliminary results of the Congregational Development survey we began in the fall of 2001. We had come up with the 10 Best Practices that we felt reflected a robust design, and we were very excited about them. Jim seemed receptive, yet in his gentle but clear-thinking way of engaging, he also said there must be more to a robust church development effort than 10 Practices. He mentioned something about people's own faith playing a role. Peter and Jim continued conversing while my mind began to wrestle with what Jim had said. I realized, as soon as he made his comment, that he was right. The 10 Best Practices were important, but they were only one element. Personal faith was as well. That left me with a hole! Faith and practices were part of it, but there was something more. I began to doodle while Jim and Peter spoke. I continued wrestling with it after the conversation ended.

Ultimately, my thinking was shaped by three questions that are progressive in nature. That is, one leads logically to the next.

1. *Why do we care about the task?*
   (Or more directly: Why do we bother?)

2. *How do we think about the task?*

3. *How do we structure our regional bodies for the task?*

This issue of personal faith raised by Jim Powell seemed to be a good place to start addressing the first question. And the 10 Best Practices did the same for the third question. But how to think about the task took some reflection. Ultimately, it occurred that we needed principles that would shape how we think about the task, and these principles needed to be objectified. And what kind of principles ought to shape our thinking? This is where much of the work being done today by missiologists enters our discussion. If the church in North America faces a missionary setting, then perhaps the way churches are shaped today needs to be informed by missiological principles. That is to say, perhaps our church development efforts need to be informed by solid missiological principles.

With these thoughts in mind, if we want our church development efforts to meet the objectives of a robust design, they will be shaped around solid answers to these questions. The answers address the three key elements of a robust effort. Each element is important, and all three are related. What are the elements? A robust effort is:

1. *built upon a Passionate Faith*

2. *shaped by Missiological Principles and*

3. *demonstrates evidence of the 10 Best Practices of church development*

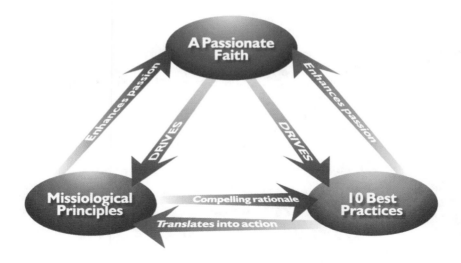

I do not think it is enough to share just the practices. While they are fundamentally important, by themselves they lack the drive that a passionate faith generates and the compelling rationale that missiological principles provide. Having said that, without the practices, the principles are nothing but ideas. The practices translate those principles into action at the regional level in support of vital congregations. And, I would also add that as people see these principles and practices enacted, their faith will be encouraged and enhanced. The three are important and interrelated as the graphic demonstrates.

Together the three elements comprise a robust design. Individually, they do not.

Conclusion

A robust effort includes faith, principles and practices. Together, these three elements are the shape of our robust church development vision. Together, they meet the objectives of a robust design. We must understand the shape of the vision before we can realize or embrace the vision. The rest of Part I of this book will unpack this vision more fully as each element is examined in more detail.

Engagement Guide

The Purpose

To engage other leaders of church development in a conversation about this chapter.

Group Discussion Questions

The Roles of Regional Bodies

It was suggested that the twin roles of a regional body are regulation and support.

> • *Do you recognize these in your regional body? How does it look in your tradition?*

> • *If you had to assign a percentage to each, what percentage is regulation and what percentage support?*

> * *Discuss your opinions of the statement that we must tilt the scales toward support. Do you agree or disagree? If you agree, do you think it is realistic in your system? If it is, what would it take? What are the obstacles?*

Your Church Development Effort

Use the notion of a dream as either wishful thinking or captivating vision as a way of thinking about your regional body's church development effort.

> • *Do you think you have a captivating vision for church development or would you describe your collective efforts more as wishful thinking? Share your thoughts and your observations.*

> • *Using the definition of a "robust effort" described in this chapter, would you say yours is robust? If yes, how so? What about it fits the criteria given? If no, what in your estimation are the reasons?*

ENDNOTES

[1] Gil Rendle of the Alban Institute (Bethesda, MD) in a report titled, "Finding the Path in the Wilderness: Middle Judicatory Case Studies and Learnings," p. 26.

[2] Ibid., p. 15.

[3] Ibid., p. 27.

[4] Bishop Claude Payne, Reclaiming the Great Commission: A Practical Model for Transforming Denominations and Congregations (San Francisco: Josey-Bass, 2000), p. 142

[5] The reader is referred to the Foreword where the determination to use the term "church development" instead of "congregational development" was explained.

A Passionate Faith

It was January 1988. I was asked to join the staff of the Presbytery of Los Ranchos to lead its mission study program. It was my first official call in the Presbyterian Church and the position that allowed me to complete my ordination process. In this newly created position, I would have the opportunity to design a new mission study process and employ it in my work with our churches.[1] It was an exciting prospect to assist the churches of my presbytery in the process of rethinking their mission. One of my current Percept partners, Mark Schulz, and I cut our "product development" teeth creating a mission planning program that would allow churches to look both at their community and their congregation and then ask some fundamental missional questions. For two years I spent on average three nights a week in churches across my presbytery leading them in a process of mission reflection.

It was an exciting time. My primary drive in ministry had been to see churches authentically engage their communities, faithfully proclaiming and practicing the Gospel in the process. Here was an opportunity to see that happen, to assist these churches to make that happen. My faith drove me into ministry and flowing out of that faith was a passion for the ministries of these churches.

In the first chapter three questions were articulated that must be answered if we would develop a robust church development effort. The first question is the topic of this chapter: Why do we care about the task? Why do you care? I believe the answer to this question and the first element of a robust effort is a "passionate faith." It was my faith that excited me in those early days on presbytery staff. I felt God's call to serve the churches of my presbytery. But not only me, I had a committee of folks, some pastors and some lay folks who shared the same passion. Once the mission study program was designed and tested, we built a team of others who also wanted to serve our churches. By the end of two years, there were several persons available to go out to the churches and facilitate a mission planning process. For each person on that team, this service was an extension of personal faith, and they too were passionate about the work and possibilities. We saw some wonderful things accomplished as several of these churches exercised the courage to look at themselves and their communities and ask some tough questions, such as: Are we representative of the community in which our campus is located? Such experiences were personally gratifying and faith uplifting. I was convinced that this was indicative of God's Spirit at work in the midst of these churches.

But to be perfectly honest, there was also some discouragement and frustration. One dear lady remarked once that she wished the presbytery would just leave her church alone until they all died and then change her church. This too is part of serving at a regional or national level.

Disconnection

Though I am sure most do not intend for this to happen, nonetheless I have noted a tendency for denominational staff to experience some disconnect from their roots in ministry. I fear at times that the intimate, personal calling that compelled many into ministry begins to be overshadowed by the day-to-day tasks one must manage at a staff level within our denominational systems. It is an unfortunate trap of ministry once one moves away from the local congregation level. And it is not just denominational staffs that struggle with this. Any of us whose ministry is primarily beyond the local church level struggles to avoid this trap. Most of us went into ministry to love and care for people, to be shepherds of a flock of God's people. But as we move into positions that are more administrative in nature, a gap begins to form between the original passion that drove us into ministry and the day to day jobs we do. Meaning no disrespect, too many staff folk find themselves devolving into bureaucratic functionaries. This is not what they want; it is too often what the job requires. This is dangerous for a robust effort. It is also dangerous to personal faith development.

Church development at a regional level can be one of those tasks where the disconnect can occur. Church development is a somewhat generic title for a host of activities carried out by a regional or national denominational body that often includes planting new churches and working with churches in decline and/or transition environments. It can also include gently nudging congregations to consider more carefully their missional responsibility as a community of faith in a particular community. Some are not very excited to do so! The work can be challenging and, at times, it can sap the life out of regional staff and volunteers. From personal experience and by way of observation, I note at least three life-sapping states that regional leadership can fall into: disappointment, disenchantment and disheartenment. Each reflects a progressive disconnection from the passionate faith with which leaders originally embraced their calling.

Disappointment

Most of us want to please and be pleased. We want to know that our efforts are worth something or accomplishing something. Yet if we are honest, at times working in church development results in frustration. Perhaps reflecting my own idealism, I simply assumed churches wanted to engage their communities, wanted to discover a renewed sense of God's calling. I confess to feelings of great disappointment when I discovered that many did not seek community engagement or a renewal, at least not at first. We used to joke about the opening statement I would make as an icebreaker. "Hi, I'm from Presbytery and I'm here to assist you!" Too often, the best I received was blank stares.

Many conversations of Percept staff with regional leaders reveal the same kinds of stories and a similar kind of disappointment. I believe it is safe to assume that most who go to work at regional or national level see in such callings an opportunity to have a broader impact. But multiple experiences of disappointment begin to sap the life out of a person. And that leads to the next state of disconnection—disenchantment.

Disenchantment

Though beginning with great expectations, too many disappointments will eventually add up to disenchantment.

The opposite of disenchantment is enchantment. I love the word "enchantment." It speaks to me of God's sovereign and sustaining presence in our world. It speaks to me of the wonder of Christ's incarnation, God become flesh and living among us. It speaks to me of the movement of the Holy Spirit in God's church. It speaks to me of the role we are called to play as instruments of God's love and grace. God enchants this unenchanted world. It is the enchantment of God that calls us to serve and that calls many of us to serve God's church in ministries beyond the local congregation, such as church development.

But constant frustration and multiple disappointments can lead to disenchantment. Wonder morphs into drudgery. Passion becomes toil.

Sacred quest becomes secular activity. There were times when it felt like doing one more meeting with a church would break me. Complaints, conflicts, positioning—all eat at the soul and disillusion one. I found the enchantment fading, and with it, more of my faith passion sapped away.

Disenchantment leads to the next state of disconnection—disheartenment.

Disheartenment

The heart is often used as a metaphor for the primary source of the human drive to live. It is the seat of the spirit, the source of courage and wellspring of hope. It is in the heart that the enchantment of God works. It is in the heart that faith is born and grows. It is the place of passion.

But it is also the place where disenchantment does its greatest harm, for it robs the heart of its faith, its courage and its hope. It leaves in its stead, disheartenment—the state in which one feels demoralized, dejected and dispirited.

Spiritual health and emotional health are related. When we feel spiritually disheartened, it is likely that emotional lowness will accompany it. I believe it is safe to say some regional leaders suffer from a mild to perhaps serious depression. Low emotional states too often translate into minimal energy to press forward with solid church development efforts. We find a fair amount of emotional lowness and perhaps even depression among regional leadership. Sometimes it manifests itself as little drive to do anything. In other settings edginess and anger express the emotional drain. Offers of assistance are met with antagonism and/or suspicion. It grieves me that persons so disheartened should lead endeavors that are particular expressions of God's mission in the world. But I am grieved even more because I know that it was not always this way. These are men and women who once heard God's call to serve and in faith embraced that call. Along the way they became disappointed, then disenchanted and now are disheartened.

I sat across from a denominational executive one day and listened as he spoke about his work situation. The office was rife with distrust and conflict. Though he worked hard and faithfully, others met his efforts with constant critique, many of whom were accomplishing little. After 30 years of service, this man who loved God and was one day called by God into ministry was practically defeated by his experiences of serving his church. His heart was nearly broken. He was disheartened. And what was worse, one sensed that there was very little passionate faith left. A significant disconnect between the faith that had responded to God's call to ministry and the ministry in which he served was very apparent. The job was still there to do, but the passionate faith that energized him to do the job was not.

It is not just clergy in non-local congregation ministry who struggle with this. Faithful lay folk whose ministry within their own congregations is recognized find themselves sitting on denominational committees seemingly far removed from the sorts of hands-on ministry that originally excited them. They attend meetings that are often dull and accomplish little. They struggle to make a connection between what so excited them in service in their local church and this new challenge of serving at the regional level. Some years ago, I listened to a laywoman vent her frustration that ever since she joined the church development committee, all she did was review "project reports." Each initiative was called a project. Committee meetings were mostly the staff person for the committee presenting project reports to them. And each meeting, the committee was given an update on the status of each project. She felt disconnected from the original passion she had enjoyed. And she wanted to resign and return to the local church where the real action was.

Regardless of your personal story, if you serve in some capacity as a leader of your regional body's church development effort and if you are at all like me, you find yourself occasionally asking the question: Why do I care about this task of developing or working with congregations? Why do I bother?

Are you passionate about the work of church development as an expression of your faith? Or are you feeling a disconnect between what you do and the faith passion that initially compelled you into ministry?

The Importance of Faith to Passion

It is always dangerous to try to intellectualize something so personal and even mystical as faith. But I believe we can do intellectual reflection and in the process better illustrate the thesis that passionate faith is the first element of a robust effort. Perhaps a good place to begin is by asking a question. What is faith? The classic text on faith in Hebrews 11 immediately comes to mind.

Now faith is the assurance of things hoped for, the conviction of things not seen. Indeed, by faith our ancestors received approval.

By faith we understand that the worlds were prepared by the word
of God, so that what is seen was made from things that are not
visible (vv. 1-3).

Biblical faith always points toward God and toward God's plans
and purposes. It always points toward a reality beyond what our normal
senses can sense. It is the expectation that God will fulfil promises made.
Faith provides us an alternate way of seeing. It is the conviction that what
is not easily discernable by the secular eye is still possible and within God's
purposes is a certainty. Faith is the way we embrace hope. Faith is the way
we enact that hope. Faith sees, faith embraces and faith enacts. Let's look
at each of these more carefully.

Faith Seeing

Scholars across many disciplines note that the great enemy and source of fear
for humans and human societies is falling into chaos—the ordered cosmos
degenerating into disorder and uncertainty.[2] Even the opening of Genesis
speaks to God as creator who shapes the cosmos out of the chaos.

In the beginning when God created the heavens and the earth,
the earth was a formless void and darkness covered the face
of the deep, while a wind from God swept over the face of the
waters. Then God said, "Let there be light"; and there was light
(vv. 1-3).

The picture is of a watery chaos with the wind of God brooding over
it. There is anticipation that something is about to happen. Then, God
speaks and order is created out of chaos. From the very beginning of the
Hebrew Scriptures, we are told that God was a God who has power over
the chaos. God speaks and order occurs.

Anthropologist Clifford Geertz explains that humans are driven to
remove the fear of chaos. But, he notes, there are three points where it
threatens nonetheless to overcome us—

1) things we can not explain—mysteries that baffle us

2) things we cannot endure—suffering

3) things whose moral solution is unclear—ethical dilemmas

It is not that we experience these things that troubles humans, it is
our fear of what they suggest, quoting Geertz, "that perhaps the world,
and hence man's life in the world, has no genuine order at all."[3]

From an anthropological standpoint, religion plays a key role in addressing this fear. How is this so? Because it provides a perspective, what Geertz calls a "religious perspective." And what is that? It is that classic statement of Augustine's: fides quaerens intellectum, "a faith in search of understanding." Geertz says, "He who would know must first believe." The readers of Genesis found a bold statement that inspired faith and gave hope that chaos would not win. For here at the very beginning of the Hebrew Bible is a statement that all that you see, everything that exists was created by God. There was a moment in the story wherein Chaos seemed to be all that was—a vast, watery abyss. But across that water the wind of God began to stir. And then God spoke and order sprang into existence. The light was separated from the darkness. A space between the waters was formed and held in place by God's word. Dry land was created by the further separation of the waters. And having created the habitats, this same God called appropriate inhabitants for each into existence. The sun, the moon and the stars were placed in their heavenly habitat. The sea animals and the birds of the air were placed in their habitats and the land animals and humans in theirs. The world was ordered. Day would follow night. The land would be fruitful and the creation would multiply. God would sustain all. Chaos did not and would not win. The story calls for a response of faith. And having believed, the reader could progress in understanding and rebut the fear of Chaos. Faith allowed the ancient Israelite and millions of believers since to rest in the knowledge that it is God's world and God sustains it and its order. One does not need to fear the chaos. One can proceed through life confident that God's order will prevail. As stated previously, Geertz calls this the religious perspective. We might also call it faith—perhaps a passionate faith.

Such a faith in God is the beginning and the source of any effort. This is because faith provides us a perspective on what is going on around us that is rooted in God's purposes in and for the world. As will be discussed in the next chapter, God has a mission in the world. Faith allows one to see traces of that mission even in the stresses and strains of life and ministry. More simply, a passionate faith provides us a way of seeing. While it may appear that chaos is swirling around us, God is the master of chaos. God can create order out of chaos.

This of course is a particular perspective, not one shared by all in our postmodern world. Indeed, a hallmark of postmodernity is the proliferation of perspectives, of points of view. While one perspective would see our world slipping inexorably into the chaos of terrorism, injustice, racism, sexism, etc., another perspective, a perspective shaped by faith sees these realities, but sees beyond them as well. A perspective shaped by faith, sees hope beyond the despair, sees the eschatological future God has promised in Christ. A perspective shaped by faith envisions the church as the temporal sign, foretaste, instrument and witness of this great hope that there is an alternative future. Faith allows us to "see" that things do not have to be this way. Faith allows us to ground our lives in the hope that chaos certainly will not win! That is a way of seeing!

The dream of Martin Luther King, Jr., was rooted in such faith. His dream was faith, seeing. It allowed him to see beyond the ugliness and injustice so many in the African-American community experienced and to envision a time when it would be different. So instead of despair, he dreamed. That was passionate faith.

Faith allows us to see life through the eyes of God's purposes and intent—a Kingdom of God perspective that believes that God will continue to faithfully complete redemption and bring healing to Creation.

Faith Embraced

Seeing things in this manner evokes trust. Faith seeing becomes faith embraced. We embrace this God who has shown us an alternative vision and hope. We place our trust in this God as the anchor of our life, as the Lord of his church and hope of the world. Faith embraced is not just ideas, not just seeing things a certain way; it is trusting the God who has given the sight.

Our vision sometimes becomes clouded by the daily challenges life presents. Some of the challenges presented by service to congregations at the regional level can cause a veil to come between our faith seeing and us. When that happens, trust wavers and hope becomes shaky. When Peter saw Jesus walking across the water toward him during the storm, he was initially filled with passionate trust and he embraced that trust, stepping out of the boat and stepping toward Jesus. But then he looked around. He saw what the secular eye sees—all it is capable of seeing—a storm, large waves and the safety of a boat some yards away. The faith he had embraced a few moments before let go and into the water he sank. But of course it is the nature of God's grace that Jesus extended his hand and embraced Peter, once again saving him from his unbelief.

By faith we believed God and embraced the hope and promise. By faith we were able to "see" what God sees when looking upon the mission of the church as the Spirit works in and through it. By faith, you and I embraced that image and responded to the call to serve. But many of us are now like Peter. We got out of the boat and we embraced the call, but then we looked around. We saw what the secular eye sees when it looks at the church and its institutions. And our hearts began to sink. Jesus is still there and his hand is still ready to grab us, to embrace us.

I believe many of us need to re-embrace the faith that called us into ministry to begin with. When we face that difficult church or the conflicted staff situation or even our own weariness, let us look again. Let us embrace again.

This idea of faith embraced will be explored more fully in the final chapter.

Faith Enacted

Finally faith seeing and faith embracing energizes. It provokes passion, a passion to act. Peter saw. Peter embraced. Peter acted. He stepped out of the boat. His faith was translated into action. Trust provokes a passion for God and God's purposes and this passion drives action. Is this not why you first responded to the call to ministry? Is this not why, when presented with the opportunity to work in church development, you said, "Yes!"

Having reviewed these thoughts about faith, consider again the first question: Why do you care about the task? Given the work involved in church development, why do you bother? I believe each of us bothered initially because a calling sprang from the deep wells of our faith. "Seeing" that is made possible because of our belief in God results in a sense of calling to participate in God's great work. That is still true. Passionate faith is faith seeing, faith embracing and faith enacted. Passionate faith gives the reason and motivation for participation in the mission of God. It gives the reason why we first cared. Passionate faith is necessary if our actions are to be more than toil. It is the first element of a robust church development effort.

Reconnection

I believe those working at the regional and national level are called to play a key role as missionary leaders for their congregations. And that calling grows directly out of their own faith commitment and passion. This passion becomes a key source of mission and the spiritual energy to engage. And it explains why we should care about the task of church development. But for many of us, this passion seems to be gone, or at least greatly diminished under the daily stresses of the job.

So, if a passionate faith is critical to a robust effort, some of us need to do some personal reflection about the spiritual condition of our faith. At some point in our life, God called and in faith we responded. If we would see robust church development efforts in our regional bodies, those of us leading in those places must reconnect with that faith passion which energized us to begin with.

Now you may be reading this and this is no problem for you. We are grateful for that. And if you believe that it is a passionate faith that drives your regional body's efforts, then you have the first element already in place. But if you are not certain, then wrestling with this is where you must begin to develop a robust effort. It is very personal and yet has communal implications. It is personal in that one's faith is something shared between God and oneself. But it is communal as well, for if as a group, one or more of us is feeling disconnected, that will impact the whole, sapping the passion out of a collective effort. Of course the opposite is also true. Where the members of an endeavor share together a passionate faith, there is the necessary energy to move efforts forward. This is what is required for a robust effort.

How are you doing? Do you feel passionate about your faith and the work to which you are called? Or do you feel disappointment, disenchanted and/or disheartened? Has the ministry become a drudgery? Do you feel like it is only a job? Do you feel emotionally down, with little energy? Do you serve in a context where political power and positioning games are more descriptive of your work than joyous service? Do you find yourself frustrated and irritated on a regular basis? To answer any of these in the affirmative is not to invite judgment. I confess to struggling with all of these at times. Rather, these questions invite you to prayer and encourage you not to stay in this place but to look for ways to move forward and to see your faith renewed.

Many leaders are becoming more aware of the crucial role one's own spiritual health plays in ministry. There are many faith-building resources available today. You may want to explore some of these with your fellow leaders. You may even want to invite someone to take you all on retreat together with the sole purpose being spiritual renewal—allowing no church development work to be done at all. Let it be a time of personal faith renewal and community building.

Let me close this brief but important chapter with a story that illustrates the power of faith to transform a job into a passion. Courtney joined Percept's staff in 2001. We had posted a new position on jobs.com for a Client Support Coordinator. The job description was written in such a way to make it clear that we worked with the church and that the job would require assisting church leaders in the effective usage of our information resources. But we set no qualifications on the job that required or even inquired about a personal faith commitment. We believed that simply indicating honestly who we were and with whom we worked would filter out those who would not want to work with the church. Courtney came. She interviewed. And we were fortunate to hire her. Subsequent conversations revealed that she was raised in the Roman Catholic Church, though her involvement had not been strong in recent years.

Initially, coming to work at Percept was just a job. It was a good job, and she enjoyed the working relationships and environment. But something began to happen to her as she learned more of what we are about and our mission of assisting the church to deal with the challenges of a changing world. She began to get to know her clients and began to care about them and their work. One day we were discussing these unfolding discoveries. She was changing and her view of her job was changing. It had grown beyond a job. This young Roman Catholic woman began to believe she had a ministry calling. Her work assisting her clients was not just a job, it was becoming an expression of a renewing faith and a passion for her work began to be evident in how she approached it.

If you asked Courtney today why she cares about the task of her clients, she would say that the mission of the church is important and she has a role to play in assisting it in that mission. A job became a passionate expression of her faith.

Conclusion

Passionate faith is the first element of a robust effort. It is the passionate faith that connects the work with the heart. Faith connects the soul with calling. It allows us to know that this work is a calling fulfilled. Passionate faith in each person involved in church development in your regional body is the energy that keeps the ministry of assisting congregations going. We will return to the matter of passionate faith again in the final chapter.

Before you proceed to the next chapter, I would ask you to reflect on the question, "Why do I bother?" Do you bother because you feel a connection to a deep, passionate faith in God and God's calling on your life? Or do you feel disconnected from your faith relative to the task of church development? Perhaps these would be good questions for some spiritual reflection, maybe some journaling. Please do not rush past it. Please avoid the trap I so often fall into of living in my head and not giving space to my heart to stop and to listen and to reflect on God and God's calling.

My prayer for you and me is this:

God, keep what we do connected to who you are and your love and acceptance of us. God keep what we do connected to your calling upon our life. Renew our faith. Allow the passion to fire us again in your service. Amen.

Engagement Guide

The Purpose

To engage in a conversation about each person's current faith experience and the impact it is having on their work.

Personal Reflection Time

Begin with some time alone. Reflect on the following questions and perhaps write your thoughts and feelings in a journal. Not all of these questions will be relevant to you. Read them through and pick out the ones that you resonate with and spend your time on them.

- *How do you feel you are you doing in your faith journey with God? Would you describe yourself today as passionate about your faith? Or do you feel disconnected?*

- *Have you struggled with disappointment in your work?*

- *Have you ever felt or do you now feel disenchanted by the work?*

- *Do you feel disheartened? Has the ministry become a drudgery? Do you feel like it is just a job? Do you feel emotionally down and with little energy?*

- *Do you serve in a context where political power and positioning games are more descriptive of the work than joyous service?*

- *Do you find yourself frustrated and irritated on a regular basis?*

As you complete your personal reflection time, imagine what you could and/or would like to share with your colleagues? How does it make you feel to even consider sharing with them?

Group Discussion Questions

The time spent alone on the personal questions is sacred. Part of the assignment was to consider what each person might want to share. During the group discussion, encourage one another to share their thoughts. Perhaps allow one another to ask clarifying questions only.

When each person has shared, ask the group what they heard.

- *Were there common themes?*

- *Were there themes that might be addressable together?*

- *Were there things you might do differently together?*

Close with a prayer for a renewed faith passion.

ENDNOTES

[1] It was really a joint project of what was to become Percept and the Presbytery of Los Ranchos. I worked half time in my staff position, and Mark Schulz and I worked the rest of the time trying to get our new consulting firm under way. Our first product, *Your Church and Its Mission* was created through this partnership. This program was superceded a few years later by ReVision.

[2] Peter Berger, The Sacred Canopy (New York: Anchor Books, 1990); Clifford Geertz, The Interpretation of Cultures (London: Hutchinson, 1975); Gerhard von Rad, Genesis, A Commentary, trans. by John H. Marks (Philadelphia: Westminster, 1972).

[3] Geertz, p. 108.

Six Principles

The last few years have seen a floodgate opened around the recognition that North America has become a primary mission field and that the churches in North America must reshape themselves into mission outposts. Books, seminars and consultations proliferate around this agenda. It is curious that we struggled for so long to know what to do with the growing recognition of our new situation. Once the challenge was articulated as a missionary task, it was as if a fog lifted and we could see clearly again. When we wrote *Death of the Church* (Zondervan, 1995), the fog was still thick and the way forward very uncertain. Theologically, we could affirm by faith that God's faithfulness would see a way forward for God's church. But most of us struggled to translate that theological affirmation into a concrete vision of churches for our new situation. Indeed, we ended the book with a statement of uncertainty and a statement of faith.

But things have changed radically since the mid-1990s. The emergence of a missiologically defined vision of the church has taken firm root—at least as a defining idea. All across North America, the missional nature of the church is being embraced. The way forward is becoming clearer, and new, more focused questions are being articulated. For example: If the church is a missionary outpost in our postmodern, post-Christian world, what will it need to look like? What biblical and theological principles should give shape to this new situation? We greatly encourage denominational leaders to aggressively engage this conversation at any level you can.

It is in this discussion that our second question is substantially addressed: How do we think about the task? As we try to rethink and reshape church development efforts around this new missionary context, what principles should be the foundation of our thinking, our shaping and ultimately, our provision of support and resources?

The Role of Principles

Why principles? Remember the second question is: How do we think about the task? Ideas give shape to endeavors. Sometimes these ideas exist unconsciously, living just under the surface but influencing us nonetheless. An example of this is the ongoing influence of a Christendom way of imaging the church's relationship to the culture. A set of ideas and beliefs has given shape to the traditional life of the church that is derived from Christendom assumptions. For too long, these assumptions have gone unchallenged. The Protestant side of the family has been discussing this, but for many it is an abstract concept. Indeed, we have discovered that among many of our Roman Catholic friends and clients, this conversation is not extensively discussed. Either way, the direct connections of Christendom assumptions to our ways of being the church in North America often go unchallenged. The result—the church's way of living and working within the culture no longer connecting with the culture. Try to change these beliefs and ideas without rooting out the underlying assumptions and change efforts will fail. Let me be more concrete. Christendom understood the role of pastor as chaplain to the congregation. He or she is called to the congregation to care for them. That is the primary job of the pastor. But in a missionary context, the role of pastor must be imaged differently. She or he must not be the chaplain to the congregation. The pastor must equip and lead the congregation in its engagement of the community. The missionary pastor builds a missionary community that engages its community missionally.

How do we challenge such unspoken assumptions? We objectify principles that we trust to shape our ways of thinking about our task. These principles then become guidelines within which we seek to give new shape and form to our efforts. They provide a different way of thinking, a new language within which to be imaginative, and which allows us to challenge the old assumptions that must be rooted out. Their very presence raises questions that might not otherwise be raised, thus allowing a status quo to prevail where it needs to be transformed. Principles are critically important. And objectively stated principles are essential to transformation.

The Six Principles

I propose six missiological principles that I believe need to shape the way we think about the task of developing and supporting missional congregations at a regional level. This list is not exhaustive. And there is certainly much rich theological reflection occurring today around the missiological challenge for the church. But these are principles that our experience has shown us to be fundamentally important in the direct work of church development as a missionary enterprise.

First Principle: God Is a Missionary God

The first missiological principle and the one upon which all church development efforts must be based is this: God is a missionary God whose mission is the inauguration and extension of God's redemptive reign. Generally considered to have been given its first expression by Karl Barth, developments in theology in the last century began to "articulate mission as an activity of God himself."[1] Rooted firmly in God's love and compassion for creation and humans in their brokenness, God has a mission in the world.[2] The late and highly respected missiologist, David Bosch says this:

> *Mission is understood as being derived from the very nature of God. It is thus put in the context of the doctrine of the Trinity, not of ecclesiology or soteriology.[3]*

From the very beginning of the biblical story, we see God taking the initiative, first as creator and sustainer and then as redeemer.

> *In the beginning...God created the heavens and the earth (Gen. 1:1).*

> *And the LORD God made garments of skins for the man and for his wife, and clothed them (3:21).*

> *While we were still weak, at the right time Christ died for the ungodly. Indeed, rarely will anyone die for a righteous person— though perhaps for a good person someone might actually dare to die. But God proves his love for us in that while we still were sinners Christ died for us (Rom. 5:6-8).*

Darrell Guder's book, *Missional Church*, provides these insights into God as a missionary God:

> *We have come to see that mission is not merely an activity of the Church. Rather, mission is the result of God's initiative, rooted in God's purposes to restore and heal creation. "Mission" means "sending", and it is the central biblical theme describing the purpose of God's action in human history. God's mission began with the call of Israel to receive God's blessings in order to be a*

blessing to the nations. God's mission unfolded in the history of God's people across the centuries recorded in Scripture, and it reached its revelatory climax in the incarnation of God's work of salvation in Jesus ministering, crucified, and resurrected. God's mission continued then in the sending of the Spirit to call forth and empower the church as the witness to God's good news in Jesus Christ. It continues today in the worldwide witness of churches in every culture to the gospel of Jesus Christ and it moves toward the promised consummation of God's salvation in the eschaton (last or final day).[4]

The foundation of the church's new self-understanding as a missionary enterprise to North America is rooted in the notion that it is God's mission. Likewise, when we begin to reconceptualize church development, we must also have our thinking originate in this principle. God is the initiator. God is the leader and sustainer. God will be the finisher. It is God's mission.

Second Principle: God Calls Us to Participate

This leads to the second principle: God calls us to participate in that mission as God's people, the church. The Church's identity is directly derived from the missio Dei, the mission of God. God has invited his people to join in that mission. Bosch again:

The classical doctrine of missio Dei as God the Father, sending the Son and God the Father and the Son sending the Spirit is expanded to include yet another "movement": Father, Son and Holy Spirit sending the church into the world.[5]

This is crystallized in the text from John 20. Here Jesus ties all of this together:

Jesus said to them again, "Peace be with you. As the Father has sent me, so I send you." When he had said this, he breathed on them and said to them, "Receive the Holy Spirit" (vv. 21-22).

Jurgen Moltman said, "It is not the church that has a mission of salvation to fulfill, it is the mission of the Son and the Spirit through the Father that includes the church."[6] Mission is first an initiative of God toward the world. And the church is sent to carry this mission of salvation throughout the world as God's representative.

Unfortunately, most of our understandings of the nature and purpose of the church were formulated within a Christendom framework. Under Christendom, the church "did" mission as one task among many. But Bosch, along with others is refocusing our understanding of the purpose and role of the Church. The church does not "do" mission as part of its institutional life. At its very core, the church "is" a missionary enterprise. Our mission is to participate in God's mission. Everything we do, therefore, must extend from God's mission and extend God's mission into God's world. We have no other business.

The mission of the church then is directly tied to God's mission in the world. The Church is the people of God sent into the world to be a sign, a foretaste, an agency and a witness to the redemptive reign of God. This is what we mean when we speak of vital and healthy congregations as mission outposts.

Seeing existing congregations reshaped around this principle and all new congregations built upon it must be the end of our work in church development. A robust effort will shape itself around the creation and support of these kinds of faith communities.

Third Principle: A Cross-Cultural Missionary Enterprise

The third missiological principle is this: Mission in twenty-first century North America is a cross-cultural missionary enterprise. This principle requires greater background discussion in order to be well understood. Most North American Christians would not image the task of the North American church as cross-cultural except perhaps where specific mission efforts are directed at particular emerging racial/ethnic communities. To make the case, we briefly review a growing gap between the traditional churched culture in North America and the larger culture—or cultures— that comprise North America today.

For much of our cultural history in North America, the churched culture and the larger culture were relatively close. But since the enlightenment, these two worlds have been separating. Initially, the separation was so minor that it was imperceptible, often only at the academic level. Throughout most of the twentieth century the larger culture began to noticeably separate from the traditional churched culture—and it did so with ever increasing speed as the century drew to a close. As we move forward into the twenty-first century, the churched culture and changing shape of American society continue to grow further apart. It is this growing gap that contributes to the reality that mission in twenty-first century North America is cross-cultural. I would raise three examples of the growing gap.

The Generational Gap

First a generation is now being born that is the third generation since the last one to consider Christianity their cultural faith and the church as part of their cultural tradition. Percept has done some generational research over the years. We found, and it is being corroborated by other research, that the two adult generations, Boomers and Survivors (genXers) are less likely to have a religious preference than previous generations. In their research, sociologists Hout and Fisher looked at the shifting religious preferences of the US population. They note a dramatic increase in the percentage of the adult population between 25 and 75 years of age who indicated no religious preference. For over 20 years, that number had remained around 7 percent. But suddenly that number had doubled to 14 percent by 1998. A partial reason for the increase of no religious preference was a generational shift. They wrote:

> The replacement of more religious cohorts with less religious cohorts can potentially explain the increase in having no religious preference: The religious did not leave their churches—cohorts that were predominately religious died or reached 75 (the age when no longer in the survey) while less religious cohorts reached age 25 (the age when they were in the survey).[7]

One generation replaced another. The former was more likely to participate in an organized religious tradition. The one that replaced it is less likely to do so.

This was emphasized when they examined the generational cohorts born after 1973. What they discovered was similar to what we have said in other venues. More children are being raised in homes where religion plays little if any part in socialization. Older Boomers were more likely to have been raised in the churched environment. Many of them upon reaching adulthood departed from active religious involvement and many never returned. Younger Boomers and Survivors were increasingly not raised in the church. Furthermore, many Boomers have not raised their children in the church. Now the Survivor generation (some of whom are the children of the older Boomers) is having children, carrying this new trend forward, also not raising their families within a religious tradition. In the early 1970s, only about 2.5 percent of American adults had been raised with no religious preference. By the late 1990s, this had increased to 6.5 percent.[8] If this trend continues, the gap between the churched culture and the emerging generations will continue to widen.

What would happen if we actually got them to come to the church? What would they experience? I believe they would be aware of the cultural gap. Our language, our values, our images, our thought structures, etc. are foreign to anyone under 35 years of age. We Boomers have some memory from childhood Sunday School, but most of us did not raise our children in the church.

The Racial/Ethnic Cultural Gap

The first gap is generational. The second reflects the increasingly diverse racial/ethnic, cultural and religious gap emerging as the face of North America changes. The census bureau projects that in the next 50 to 60 years there will be no racial-ethnic majority in the US. The fastest growing racial/ethnic population comes from Asia. In many large urban centers, the largest percentage is Hispanic/Latino. And these two broad categories mask a rich and diverse cultural world.

Now this may not be news to you, if you have been doing your homework. But this is where contextual analysis becomes critical. We start with the demographics but we must stretch beyond the numbers. These are real people, many of whom come from very different cultures, with very different beliefs and values as well as languages. And while many of us will celebrate this growing diversity, I have noticed that the celebration is often abstract. It is much harder to come to grips with this growing cultural gap on a personal, everyday, in-my-community, level.

The Worldview Gap

There is a third gap reflected in a shifting cultural phenomenon that may escape our direct awareness. The first two deal with demographic shifts. This manifestation exists at the level of ideas—specifically the underlying assumptions people hold about the nature of truth and reality. Christian mission at its core—and here I will reveal a portion of my worldview—is about telling God's story. Implicit is the belief that it is a true story. Also implicit is that if it is true, then there might be stories that are not true. The more extreme forms of postmodern thought would feel that what I just wrote is unacceptably limiting. They would like to say "not true," but extreme postmodern thought cannot say such things. In other writings I have noted that we live in a world where there are many stories, but no single story.[9] The idea of truth has been relativized. Truth does not exist. Our truth stories—including religion—are helpful fictions we invent to make sense of our world. Truth stories are simply instruments we use to accomplish our desires.

Of course there are those on the other end of the spectrum: We are not telling God's story. We are declaring the TRUTH of God—truth in capital letters with little room for questions or discussion. People of this persuasion further entrench themselves in a naïve absolutism—the home turf of all forms of fundamentalism—Christian or otherwise.

There is a middle position between these two extremes. Truth exists, and though we are limited in our ability to fully know it, we can know something and know it truly if not perfectly and completely.

What is my point? Quite simply, there is no common language of discourse. There are "many languages." Communicability between them is separated by a growing gap. For even people ostensibly speaking the same language, there is incommunicability because of the assumptions held about what is true and real.

A good friend of mine is a political conservative who hosts a call-in radio show. I tune in occasionally, just to hear what is being said—but not too often because the program drives me out of my mind. Recently I heard a person talking about dust on the moon. He explained that if the moon were 4 billion years old, as scientists insist, then there should have been enough dust on the surface to bury the lunar lander when it touched down. We all know it did not sink. Rather, he pointed out, it sank as much as one would expect if the moon were 8,000 years old.

I would not know what to say to this person. I understand his English words but I cannot communicate directly with him about the world in which we live. Based upon his naïve absolutism and its approach to the Bible, his assumptions about the nature of reality and truth create a gap between us. With each day and more scientific discoveries, the gap grows.

There are multiple perspectives about truth, especially religious truth. We cannot assume we can just speak and people will understand us. There is a growing gap created by the loss of a common language of discourse about truth.

The Cross-Cultural Gap in the Early Church

The early church faced its own challenge due to a cultural gap. As we all know, the first Christians were Palestinian Jews raised in a Jewish cultural milieu with all of the normal and expected ritual and lifestyle practices that accompanied their culture. It was not long, however, before they experienced a cultural gap. For as soon as the Gospel began to penetrate gentile communities, these practices became a problem—a cross-cultural problem. If the Gospel was to continue to move out across the world, the leaders of the early church would need to address this. This is not the place for an extended exposition on this but some comments may be helpful.

The first church council recorded in Acts chapter 15 tells the story of how it was handled. The center of the controversy is introduced in the first verse.

> Then certain individuals came down from Judea and were teaching the brothers, "Unless you are circumcised according to the custom of Moses, you cannot be saved" (v. 1).

Paul and Barnabus were quite concerned about this teaching so they were sent to Jerusalem to consult with the Apostles and Elders there. Upon arrival, they first reported the wonderful things that were happening among the gentiles. But they were immediately hit with this challenge.

> But some believers who belonged to the sect of the Pharisees stood up and said, "It is necessary for them to be circumcised and ordered to keep the law of Moses" (v. 5).

Two cultures at odds with each other. The very mission to the Gentiles hung in the balance. If the early church had insisted on what these believers from the Pharisees demanded, the mission may have failed. Paul understood this. He understood the cultural plurality represented in the growing young church. He understood and was able to distinguish between culture and the core Gospel story. And he was able to cross between both cultures. Paul's argument won over James, the brother of Jesus who evidently was the head of the Jerusalem church. For he stood and made this declaration.

> "This agrees with the words of the prophets, as it is written, 'After this I will return, and I will rebuild the dwelling of David, which has fallen; from its ruins I will rebuild it, and I will set it up, so that all other peoples may seek the Lord—even all the Gentiles over whom my name has been called.
>
> Thus says the Lord, who has been making these things known from long ago.' Therefore I have reached the decision that we should not trouble those Gentiles who are turning to God, but we should write to them to abstain only from things polluted by idols and

from fornication and from whatever has been strangled and from blood"(vv. 15-20).

And with this, the Gospel was allowed to cross cultures. I believe we face a similar sort of challenge today. That there is a growing cultural gap between the traditional churched culture and the diverse cultures that comprise North America has been demonstrated. The question for those of us from within the traditional churched culture is this: Will we recognize this gap and will we allow ourselves to build a bridge across the gap? This is our missionary setting. It is cross-cultural. If we would be faithful to our calling, we must embrace this fact and do the work as modeled for us by the early church when it faced a similar challenge.

There are multiple implications of this growing cultural gap. But one of great significance for church development is the growing realization that church development is not just a missionary enterprise. It is a cross-cultural missionary enterprise. That is to say, many of the learnings the missionary movement discovered, rather painfully about taking the Gospel into new cultures now apply to our North American context. As the racial/ethnic diversity of our nation grows and as more generations are born separate from the churched culture environment, the gap between church and culture grows, making the missionary challenge more complicated. Within North America, local congregations must learn how to build bicultural bridges between their cultural and religious experience and that of the communities around them if they hope to engage them.

For this to occur they will need resources that help them understand how to do this and that will assist them in the doing. This too must be an element of a robust church development effort.[10]

Fourth Principle: Contextual Analysis Is Critical

This leads to the fourth missiological principle: Contextual analysis is critical to effective engagement.

What do these three gaps mean? They mean, quite frankly, that we must do some homework. First we recognize and embrace the reality that ours is a cross-cultural environment. That being the case, as Church leaders, we must learn to explore and understand our particular missionary context. We need to give serious effort to studying our increasingly diverse culture. We must work to understand its way of thinking and explore its many faceted belief systems. This is in part where demographics become important. Percept got into the demographics business because we were trying to help our clients (my presbytery at the time) gain a better understanding of real people. Too many churches simply allow themselves the luxury of believing they know who is out there. Our experience over 15 years suggests that in many cases they do not. This is why contextual analysis is so critical.

When I think about this principle, I often recall Jesus' conversation with the woman at the well.

> So he came to a Samaritan city called Sychar, near the plot of ground that Jacob had given to his son Joseph. Jacob's well was there, and Jesus, tired out by his journey, was sitting by the well. It was about noon. A Samaritan woman came to draw water, and Jesus said to her, "Give me a drink." (His disciples had gone to the city to buy food.) The Samaritan woman said to him, "How is it that you, a Jew, ask a drink of me, a woman of Samaria?" (Jews do not share things in common with Samaritans.) (John 4:5-9).

Jesus met her on her turf. He fully understood her life situation including the fact that as a Samaritan, she should not have been allowed to have discourse with him. And we read later in the story that Jesus was quite aware of who she was—namely that she had had several husbands and the one with whom she currently lived was not her husband. But he was not put off by her; instead he offered her the promise of living water.

> Jesus answered her, "If you knew the gift of God, and who it is that is saying to you, 'Give me a drink,' you would have asked him, and he would have given you living water." The woman said to him, "Sir, you have no bucket, and the well is deep. Where do you get that living water? Are you greater than our ancestor Jacob, who gave us the well, and with his sons and his flocks drank from it?" Jesus said to her, "Everyone who drinks of this water will be thirsty again, but those who drink of the water that I will give them will never be thirsty. The water that I will give will become in them a spring of water gushing up to eternal life." The woman said to him, "Sir, give me this water, so that I may never be thirsty or have to keep coming here to draw water" (vv. 10-15).

Jesus knew this woman and he understood her situation. He brought the good news to her in her context, because he understood her context. She would have never heard this good news, had he not gone to her and engaged her in her life setting. I believe this story powerfully illustrates the principle of contextual analysis. The term sounds terribly academic, but the practice does not need to be. In practice, the principle means church leaders must do the work of listening and understanding if they hope to communicate.

If we understand that ours is a cross-cultural missionary setting, then our congregations must become skilled in the art of contextual analysis. Instead of trying to get the unchurched into our churches, maybe we ought to encourage our churches to get out among the people and explore their world through the eyes of their faith and within the framework of God's mission in the world. Our churches must learn how to read and interpret the culture. To do this, they will need both good contextual information resources and training in the skills of effectively interpreting these resources. We call all such activities various forms of "listening." Church leaders must become committed to, and effective at, listening.

My wife and I were attending a Donor Appreciation event for a transitional housing agency we support. Attending was a couple I had known for years from my service on the school board. At various times they had dropped hints of having once been actively involved in the church but were so no longer. I have a personal interest in exploring how people become "dechurched."[11] So, I decided to simply ask them to tell me their story. Why were they not involved? What had happened? It was a story of disillusionment and pain. Events had occurred that drove a wedge between them and the church and ultimately their faith. I just listened. I offered nothing by way of rebuttal or rationalization or even solace. I just listened. At one point, Sally admitted that she had wondered if she should reconsider, but had not yet done so. Perhaps she will some day soon. The conversation ended with us all agreeing that we needed to extend the discussion.

This is a simple illustration of listening. "Listening" can take many shapes. Listening can be a conversation. Listening can involve reading local news. Listening can include studying a demographic report. Listening in its various forms can and should be a way of doing contextual analysis.

Taking this a step forward and making a habit of listening is to practice systematic listening. Systematic listening is not something one does once—get a report, read it and set it aside. Systematic listening is an ongoing, progressive dialogue with the culture—locally, regionally and globally. We must constantly do the work of analyzing our context if we hope to speak meaningfully to it and live authentically in it as witnesses to the redemptive love of God.

Too often we have heard the comment, "Well, we did Percept already so there is nothing else we need from them." I am not quite certain what people mean when they say they did Percept, but the comment suggests that looking at one's community is something you do once and then go on about your work. That might be fine if communities were static—I do not really believe it would ever be fine—but they are not static, especially not today in any urban setting. The main reason Percept converted to an "always up-to-date, everywhere accessible" approach to delivering information was tied directly to the need of church leadership to constantly monitor what is going on in a community or region.

A robust church development effort will not only model continual contextual analysis in its own planning, it will provide opportunities for local leaders to have access to contextual information and the training to skillfully use it to listen to their communities.

Fifth Principle: Translate the Story

But listening is just the first aspect of contextual analysis. The fifth missiological principle is this: Our church leaders must also become skilled at the art of translating the Gospel story into meaningful terms, images and symbols for the culture they are trying to reach. Lamin Sanneh[12] has focused our thoughts on the need to translate the Gospel story into language and images for a particular culture. For too long we have required people to come to us and hear us express the biblical story in our language, with our symbols and using our images. I am not saying we abandon these. However, we can not expect twenty-first century people to understand them.

We must do the work of translation. This is hard work. Most would prefer that the people we are trying to reach do all the work. When we insist that worship look a certain way, that language be construed in ways that make us comfortable, we are making the culture do the work. When we build church facilities that focus on us, we are making the culture do the work. When we speak "church" or "Christian" speak, we are making the culture do the work. Shame on us. It is our job to reflect on the Gospel story and look for ways to shape its telling in forms and images of the target culture.

We had been invited to join some friends at a banquet to raise funds for a Christian mission that did incredible work with handicapped persons all over the world. The heart and compassion that drove the mission was very evident. Our host was a top executive for a major auto manufacturer. The executive and his wife had hosted a table because they believed in the social work element of the mission. The executive had also invited some of his staff. Two were a man and his son who had come to hear John Wooden, legendary coach of UCLA, speak. They were both Jewish. To my right was a young couple of no church background at all. When the program began, I knew we were in trouble for the "Christian talk" began immediately. And it was of a very particular conservative and evangelical nature. Had the room been filled only with people of faith, it might have been alright. But it was not and they knew it! At the end of the evening, the moderator of the program said, almost as an afterthought, that some in the audience "might not be Christians." He invited them to come up, and he would tell them how to become one. It was a classic example of our failure to translate, to even try to speak in language outside our own world. I do not believe these folks even knew how else to talk. No one appeared to even challenge them about their language. The non-churched folks next to me were simply bewildered and wondered how they had ended up in such a setting. They looked for the first inconspicuous moment to leave. I was actually relieved for them once they were gone.

Scripture provides many subtle examples of this principle. I say subtle because it is never really the focus of teaching so much as a missionary model exemplified in practice. One good example is the story of Paul the Apostle before the Areopagus in Athens. As Luke tells the story, Paul was waiting in Athens for Silas and Timothy. As was clearly his practice, he walked the city and looked at their cultural and religious art and expressions. And every day he would go to the marketplace to engage the people of Athens—whoever happened to be there at the time. Some Epicurean and Stoic philosophers invited him to speak with them.

> So they took him and brought him to the Areopagus and asked him, "May we know what this new teaching is that you are presenting? It sounds rather strange to us, so we would like to know what it means" (Acts 17:19-20).

Paul stands before this body and says,

> "Athenians, I see how extremely religious you are in every way. [23]For as I went through the city and looked carefully at the objects of your worship, I found among them an altar with the inscription, 'To an unknown god.' What therefore you worship as unknown, this I proclaim to you. [24]The God who made the world and everything in it, he who is Lord of heaven and earth, does not live in shrines made by human hands, [25]nor is he served by human hands, as

though he needed anything, since he himself gives to all mortals life and breath and all things. ²⁶From one ancestor he made all nations to inhabit the whole earth, and he allotted the times of their existence and the boundaries of the places where they would live, ²⁷so that they would search for God and perhaps grope for him and find him—though indeed he is not far from each one of us. ²⁸For 'In him we live and move and have our being'; as even some of your own poets have said,

'For we too are his offspring.'" (vv. 22b-28).

Paul's earlier contextual analysis—the identification of the altar to an unknown god—is used as a cultural bridge to the Athenians. He begins with them and with their culture. He continues then to speak about this god by connecting him to the God for whom he speaks. But most telling of his willingness to translate is the fact that he even quotes one of their philosophers but infuses it with theological meaning consistent with the Gospel.

"For 'In him we live and move and have our being'; as even some of your own poets have said'" (v. 28). This is translation.

Perhaps an example would be helpful. I was asked to assist a presbytery in assessing the viability of one of its new church starts. It had been started a couple of years earlier and the mission design called for it to have reached a certain membership threshold, but it was short of that target. Additionally, from one quarter rose a criticism that it was not "Presbyterian enough" and that was why it had not grown to the level targeted. My task was to provide an outside opinion of its viability. As part of the consulting engagement, I attended Sunday morning worship. Now I am not one who personally likes the more contemporary, seeker-oriented approaches but it did not take me long to sense the life and vitality that was present as those 140-plus people began to worship. They were sitting around tables. There was a professional looking multi-media presentation going on along with the worship band. (I found out later that the pastor's 14-year-old daughter had done the graphics!) Mothers were dancing in the aisles with their children and drinks and donuts were still served during worship. Was it very "Presbyterian?" Well, what is Presbyterian? We are the denomination whose creed is "Reformed, always Reforming." Clearly this church had reformed its worship and clearly it was not as one would traditionally expect to experience Presbyterian worship! But they clearly were translating the Gospel story into meaningful language and images for that culture. I later found out that over 70 percent of that young congregation had not been involved in a church prior to the church's formation.

A robust church development effort will insist on the application of the translation principle and provide training and resources necessary to integrate it into the ministries of local congregations.

Sixth Principle: Missionary Leadership Required

All of these principles depend upon one last one. Missionary leadership is required at every level of the church. Missionary leadership is a broad and extensive conversation. We cannot explore it here. But we can point to the essential quality of it. It is leadership that has rediscovered and seeks to fully embrace the apostolic function of sending and being sent. Is this not the primary thrust the author of Ephesians is trying to make?

> *The gifts he gave were that some would be apostles, some prophets, some evangelists, some pastors and teachers, to equip the saints for the work of ministry, for building up the body of Christ, until all of us come to the unity of the faith and of the knowledge of the Son of God, to maturity, to the measure of the full stature of Christ (Eph. 4:11-13).*

Christ gave leadership gifts to the church to prepare the church to carry out its mission. Church leadership is not primarily about caring for the people who are members of the church, as if they were something different than the church. Church leadership is a gift given to the church—the members—to enable them to carry out together God's mission in their communities. Local church leadership must understand that their role is to prepare the congregation as a whole and as individuals to be missionaries to the culture, empowering them with the skills and knowledge necessary to fulfill their calling. And then, send them.

Likewise, our denominational systems need to reconfigure their concept of the church leader and empower them with the skills and knowledge necessary to fulfill their calling of preparing to send others. And then send them and support them in their being sent.

A robust church development effort will take the lead in transforming our models of church leadership, for without the new model, vital congregations are not likely to emerge or develop.

The Principles and Church Development

Now you may be wondering how these principles directly relate to a robust church development effort. They seem more applicable to the way a local congregation shapes itself than how we conceive of the work of church development at a regional or national level. It is true that the more direct application of these principles is the local setting. But from the perspective of regional church development efforts, what should be the principles that guide how you assist and/or shape the mission of a local congregation? When you imagine a new church development project, what ideas should inform that effort? Is it the old unspoken notion of extending the denominational franchise? Should it be looking for places where "our people" can be found? These principles, I believe, will very directly influence how you think about the task of developing congregations regardless of the particular tradition you represent.

Conclusion

In this chapter, we have considered the second element of a robust church development effort. It is one that is shaped by theological principles of mission. These principles shape the way we think about the task. We have been called by God to participate with God in God's mission in North America today. To do so, we must recognize that ours is a cross-cultural mission context that requires listening and analysis if we are to fulfill the mission God has given to us. And it requires that we do the work of translating between our core story and the culture. It is our responsibility to bridge the gap. And this takes church leadership at every level of our church institutions that understand the missional mandate and are committed to fulfilling it.

We have now looked at the second of three elements of a robust effort. Passionate faith we believe must be informed by missiological principles. The next element focuses on how to structure a robust regional church development effort.

Engagement Guide

The Purpose

To engage in a conversation about the six missiological principles outlined in this chapter and consider how they could or should influence the way your regional body thinks about church development.

Group Discussion Questions

Role of principles

- *The chapter makes the argument that ideas give shape to endeavors. What ideas do you feel shape your church development effort? Are these ideas spoken or unspoken?*

- *Do you have a set of principles that guide your effort?*

Look at the six principles reviewed in this chapter (and repeated at the bottom of this page)

- *What is your general reaction to them?*

- *Do you think some or all of these principles already directly or indirectly influence how you think about the work of church development?*

- *Which ones do not influence how you think about the task? Why? (Haven't thought about them? Don't agree with them? Etc?)*

- *What do you think you should do with these principles? Will you let them shape the way you think about church development in your regional body?*

The Six Principles (for quick reference)

1. *God is a missionary God, whose mission is the inauguration and extension of the redemptive reign of God.*
2. *God calls us to participate in that mission as God's people, the church.*
3. *Mission in twenty-first century North America is a cross-cultural missionary enterprise.*
4. *Contextual analysis is critical to effective engagement.*
5. *It is the church's responsibility to translate.*
6. *Missionary leadership is required at each level of the church.*

ENDNOTES

[1] David Jacobus Bosch, Transforming Mission: Paradigm Shifts in Theology of Mission (Maryknoll, NY: Orbis Books, 1991), p. 389.

[2] Darrell L. Guder, The Continuing Conversion of the Church (Grand Rapids, MI: W. B. Eerdmans, 2000).

[3] Bosch, Transforming Mission, p. 390

[4] Darrell L. Guder, Missional Church (Grand Rapids, MI: W. B. Eerdmans, 1998), p. 4

[5] Bosch, Transforming Mission, p. 390.

[6] Ibid., p. 390.

[7] Hout and Fisher, ASA, p. 182.

[8] Hout and Fisher, ASA, p. 169.

[9] Mike Regele, Mark Schulz (contributor), The Death of the Church (Grand Rapids, MI: Zondervan, 1995).

[10] Paul G. Hiebert, Anthropological Reflections on Missiological Issues (Grand Rapids, MI: Baker Book House, 2001).

[11] Mary Tuomi Hammond, The Church and the Dechurched (St. Louis: Chalice Press, 2001).

[12] Lamin Sanneh, Translating the Message (Maryknoll, NY: Orbis Books, 1989).

The 10 Best Practices: The Search

What does it take for a regional leader to do an effective and successful job of developing congregations? This is an important question, but one that is not often asked. Books are released daily that focus locally on how to develop churches. Church growth has focused for years on methods and means of building a church. Church planting books are plentiful. There are books that discuss the important task of reshaping a church's ministry for a changing urban environment. But we believe there has been a big hole in all such discussions. Within denominational traditions, the development of congregations, whether new church plants or redevelopment of churches in changing contexts is generally conducted by a regional agency. Most efforts revolve around a combination of professional regional staff and volunteers who serve on church development committees. Where are the books or the conversations that provide these entities insight and guidance in their task? Indeed, what is their task? If they were asked to identify the primary activities that encompass their mission, where would they go for advice? Where are the descriptions of the regional leaders' practices that reflect effective church development efforts? Certainly there are a number of tasks that are generally considered part of the mission of church development. But is there anything that would suggest the most important things to do at a regional level that would actually shape the work of church development?

Percept began wrestling with these questions explicitly in the fall of 2001. At about that time Reverend Claire Burkat, Mission Director for the New Jersey and Southeastern Pennsylvania Synods (ELCA) and Roy Oswald of The Alban Institute released a book looking at similar questions. In the information about their book, the same point was made. I quote:

> *Transformation of the mainline denomination can begin at any structural level but the...Regional Church Body is one that has*

been sadly neglected. There are scores of books on revitalization of congregations, but the role of a Regional Church Body in such transformational work remains largely unclear and unexamined. Sorely lacking is a strategic vision for how a Regional Church Body can engage in such congregational rejuvenation.... [1]

It is to address these issues that they wrote their book, "Transformational Regional Bodies."

Like Burkat and Oswald, our experience would suggest that such support and guidance is missing. As a result, hundreds of such committees across the country are struggling desperately to conduct their work in a meaningful fashion. We suspect that many feel uncertain about where to focus their efforts. For some, this translates into doing too many things, most poorly. For others, the uncertainty paralyzes. In the face of such uncertainty, leaders get caught in an endless loop of talk but see very little in the way of accomplishment. There may be dreams of good efforts, but too often the dreams are only wishful thinking.

This state of affairs is unfortunate on its own merits. But we must also add to the problem the fact that an effective or what we would call a "robust" church development effort is critical to the future of these church traditions at this point in their history. Membership is declining. Churches are dying. Meanwhile, the United States continues to grow both in numbers and in its racial/ethnic diversity calling for many new and diverse kinds of congregations. No other effort should be of greater import under such conditions.

Combine these two realities—lack of clarity about the task and the cultural challenge the church faces today—and it becomes very clear that regional agencies and their church development efforts need some assistance in better defining the task. Such a definition must provide a framework within which they can focus and shape their efforts. There is little time or space for wasted pursuits or unhelpful emphases. They need to know what is important and what works. And they need to then focus their energies around reshaping their efforts to conform to this. A robust church development effort is critical to the future of these denominational traditions.

A National Study of Congregational Development

Toward that end, we initiated a search. We purposed to understand the current state of congregational development and how it is practiced across the United States. To accomplish this purpose, we fielded a large survey to our client family. The first part of our search provided us a good description of "what is," relative to how church development is practiced across the United States and across many different denominational traditions. Our search uncovered some good points and some unfortunate findings. But the larger goal of our search was the hope that in the data we would uncover indications of a set of best practices of church development.

As Mark Schulz and I pored over the findings, we wrestled with two questions.

1. *Is there a way to discern in the data those practices that are indicative of a robust church development effort?*

2. *And, once articulated, do those practices have the potential to transform regional level church development efforts if implemented?*

Our hope was to extract from that information a set of best practices, that if implemented, could revitalize church development efforts across our family of clients. When we fielded the survey, we were not certain what we would find. But what we found was very powerful. There are practices out there in various places in various denominational traditions that fit the definition of robust outlined in chapter one.

For the purposes of readability and in the service of clarity, we have decided to divide the general findings of the search and the best practices we discovered into two chapters. This chapter is descriptive. That is, it provides a description of the current state and practices of church development across Percept's client family. The next chapter will unveil the 10 Best Practices we discovered. By their very nature, these are offered as a prescription for how to structure a regional body to effect a robust effort for developing congregations.

Key Findings

Let's proceed now to look at some of the key findings. What is the current state of church development across the United States? While there were several categories explored, a review of nine will provide us with a pretty good picture. The nine categories include:

1. *Commitment*

2. *Critical Practices*

3. *Approaches to Planning*

4. *New Church Development*

5. *Redevelopment*

6. *Challenges*

7. *Staffing*

8. *Preparing Leadership*

9. *Financial Support*

1. Commitment

The first category looked at a regional body's commitment to congregational development. Is there one and if so, what is the level of that commitment and is the commitment growing or declining?

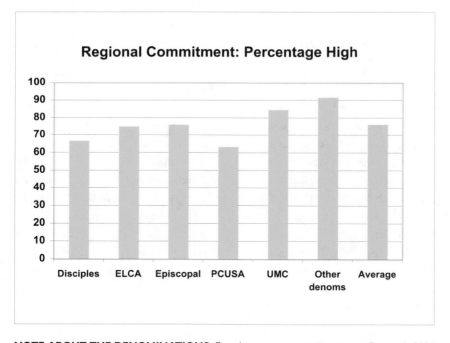

NOTE ABOUT THE DENOMINATIONS: Five denominations participating in Percept's 2001 Survey of Congregational Development had a large enough sample size to make statistically valid comparisons. They are listed here by the abbreviation/label used in the charts and graphs in Chapters 4 and 5: **Disciples** [Christian Church (Disciples of Christ)]; **ELCA** [Evangelical Lutheran Church in America]; **Episcopal** [The Episcopal Church]; **PCUSA** [Presbyterian Church (USA)]; and, **UMC** [United Methodist Church]. There were a total of twelve denominations represented. For further details about the survey refer to our website at ***www.Percept.info***.

Level of Commitment Within Regional Body

Respondents were asked to indicate how high the commitment to congregational development was within their regional body. Nearly three out of four indicated that it was high.

However, this averaging obscures some diversity denominationally. In the category of other denominations is found the greatest commitment of over 90 percent. Second to this group falls the United Methodist Church wherein 85 percent of those responding indicated that their regional commitment was high.

The weakest commitment regionally is found among the Presbyterian Church (USA) at 63 percent and the Christian Church (Disciples of Christ) at 67 percent.

The size of a regional body appears to have some influence on commitment level. For those with 200 churches or less, the commitment hits about 70 percent. But for the larger bodies, the commitment jumps 15 points to over 85 percent.

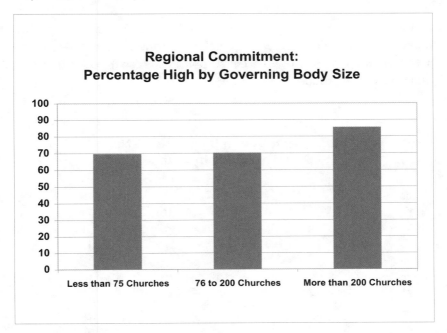

Change in Commitment

Perhaps of equal value is the direction respondents felt the commitment was moving within their governing bodies. Was it growing, declining or simply standing still? Across all respondents, nearly 65 percent indicated

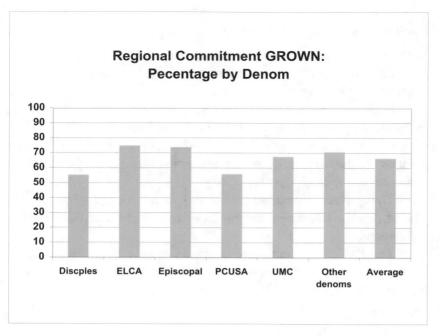

that they felt the commitment had grown in the past two years. Only 8 percent felt it had declined. But again, the more interesting story is found in the denominational cuts wherein 20-point shifts can be found between denominational groups.

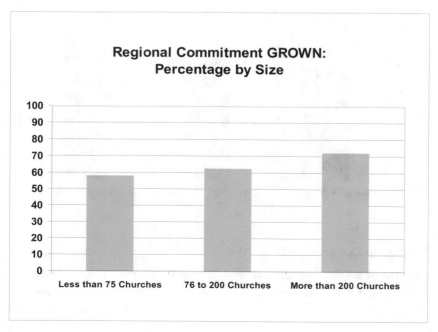

Lutherans (ELCA) and Episcopalians are more likely to believe the commitment has grown. Conversely, Presbyterians (PCUSA) are more likely to feel it has declined.

Size of regional body seems to have some bearing on the growth or decline of commitment. As the graph shows, the smaller the regional body, the less likely it was to have seen the commitment grow.

Factors Contributing to the Growth

Why would a commitment have grown or declined? First we consider factors that might have contributed to a growth in commitment.

Leadership emerges as the most important factor in church development. It is leadership with the capacity to guide efforts and move them forward that is considered the top reason for growth in the regional commitment. Nearly three in four respondents who felt the commitment had grown identified leadership capacity. We will see the leadership theme emerge many times in the analysis.

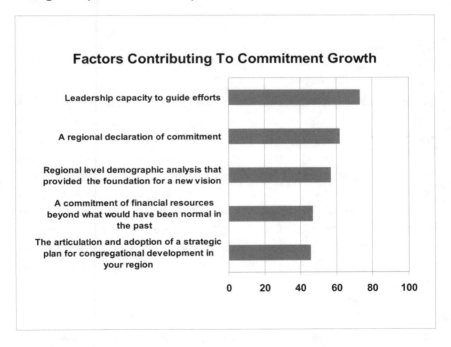

Additionally, making a public declaration of commitment is also considered a factor driving growth in regional commitments. And, we were glad to see that nearly 57 percent felt that a regional-level analysis of the regional body's demographics contributed to the formation of a new

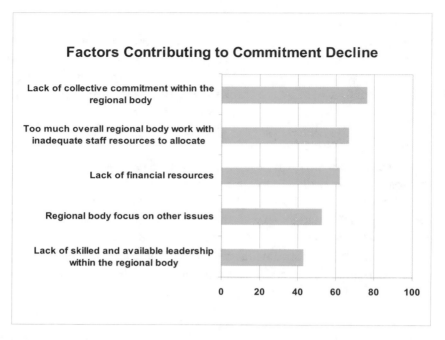

Factors Contributing to Commitment Decline

vision, which in turn energized the regional commitment.

Factors Contributing to the Decline

In some settings, the commitment to congregational development was actually declining. The graph above shows the factors that contribute to the decline.

It is not surprising that the number-one reason why the commitment to church development in regional governing bodies declined is a lack of collective commitment. In reality, this factor is probably joined with the second—too much work and not enough staff. Too few people spread too thin. Not surprisingly, financial resources were a factor. But note the last two. First is distraction. The regional body is focused on other issues. And the second is directly linked to this lack of focus—a lack of skilled leadership.

2. Critical Practices

The second category focuses on critical practices. The survey explored the kinds of activities that respondents felt were inclusive of church development. It also considered the different ways the task is conducted. For example, was it conducted through coaching, making policy, fund raising, research, etc.? The section concluded by asking respondents to

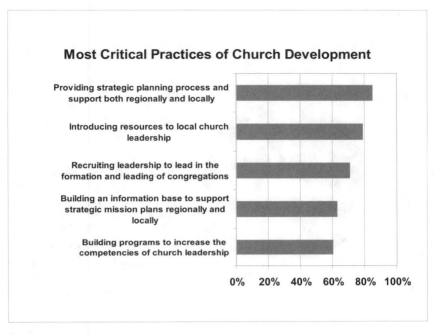

Most Critical Practices of Church Development

Providing strategic planning process and support both regionally and locally

Introducing resources to local church leadership

Recruiting leadership to lead in the formation and leading of congregations

Building an information base to support strategic mission plans regionally and locally

Building programs to increase the competencies of church leadership

0%   20%   40%   60%   80%   100%

check all practices on a list that they felt were critical.

Clearly the most important practice, at 85 percent, is providing strategic planning process and support. The item points both locally and regionally. The practice includes assisting local congregations to plan strategically. It also includes regional-level planning. A close second is introducing resources to local church leaders. A third sees the leadership issue rise again, this time in finding leaders to form new congregations. And note the last one, again related to leadership. Sixty percent feel it is critical to have programs that will increase the competencies of church leadership.

3. Approaches to Planning

The third category looks at how regional bodies approach planning—if they do. Options range from not planning to carefully executing outlined planning cycles. We will look first at the general approach to planning at the regional level followed by focusing in on planning specifically for church development.

General Regional Level Planning

First, how in general do regional bodies approach planning? From the standpoint of good planning practices, the approach to planning that sets a schedule for both strategic and annual planning and budgeting is the most

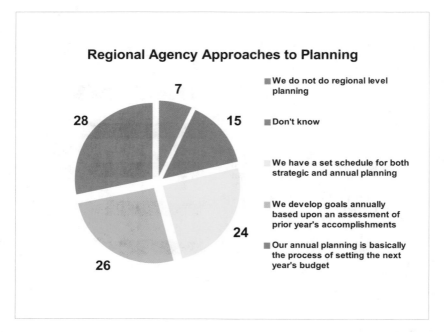

Regional Agency Approaches to Planning

7

28

15 ■ Don't know

■ We do not do regional level planning

■ We have a set schedule for both strategic and annual planning

■ We develop goals annually based upon an assessment of prior year's accomplishments

24

26

■ Our annual planning is basically the process of setting the next year's budget

comprehensive practice. The poorest practice is not doing regional level planning at all. And a true problem practice is to have people participating in regional level church development work who simply do not know if or how the regional body does regional level planning. Nearly 15 percent fall in this last category.

Only one in four agencies represented in the survey approach regional planning in what would be considered a good planning practice-focusing on both strategic and annual planning within a schedule. The next step down is to at least assess prior year accomplishments and set goals for an upcoming year accordingly, including the budget. An additional one in four employs this method.

But the highest overall percentage reduces planning to the annual process of setting the budget. I believe this is a poor practice because it lacks comprehensiveness. But even worse, it puts the ongoing scarcity of resources in the driver's seat instead of intentional mission planning and prioritization. Twenty-eight percent of all respondents indicated that this was the method of their regional body.

Of course the poorest practice is not doing regional planning. Seven percent of respondents indicated this was the practice of their regional body.

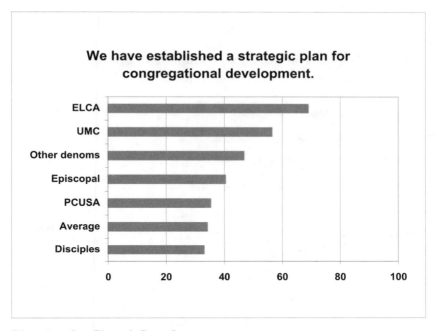

We have established a strategic plan for congregational development.

Planning for Church Development

Having observed how regional bodies generally approach planning, we turn our focus to how regional bodies specifically approach planning for church development. Respondents were given a list of four statements and asked to check all that were true. It is most revealing, I believe, when we look by denomination at the percentage checked for each item on the list.

Statement One: We have established a strategic plan for congregational development.

Of those regional agencies who have established a strategic plan for congregational development, only those from the Evangelical Lutheran Church in America (ELCA) and the United Methodist Church (UMC) have exceeded 50 percent. On the other end of the scale fall the Christian Church (Disciples) and the Presbyterian Church (PCUSA). Only one in three regional agencies within these two denominations has developed a strategic plan.

Statement Two: We have set congregational development goals for starting new churches.

Of those regional agencies that have set goals for starting new

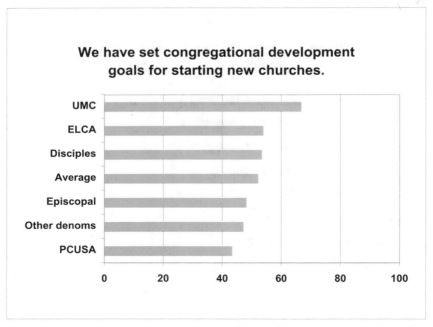

churches, again it is the United Methodists and Lutherans (ELCA) that are out front, though they have switched places, with two out of three United Methodist conferences having set goals. Bringing up the rear are the Presbyterians (PCUSA) and the Episcopalians.

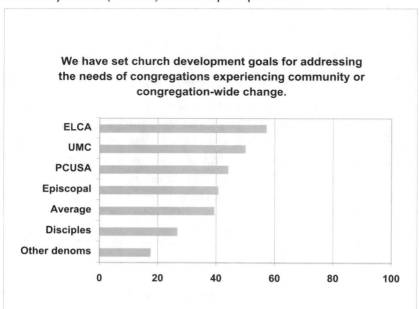

Statement Three: *We have set congregational development goals for addressing the needs of congregations experiencing community or congregation-wide change (often referred to as redevelopment and increasingly, as church transformation).*

Though the overall percentages are lower for this item, it is again the Lutherans (ELCA) and United Methodists that are out front, both exceeding 50 percent of the regional agencies represented. On this item the Presbyterians have moved up to third place.

Statement Four: *We have set goals for starting and building churches that reflect the racial/ethnic profile within our bounds.*

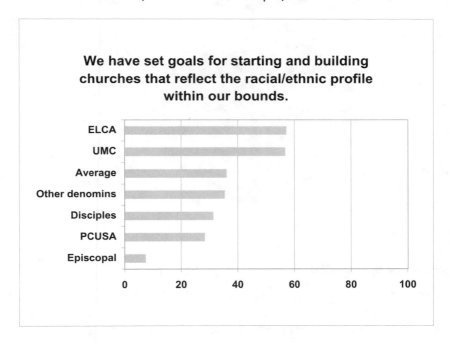

Only the Lutheran (ELCA) and United Methodist regional agencies represented in the survey have set goals for racial/ethnic church development in excess of 50 percent. Only 7 percent of the Episcopal dioceses represented have racial/ethnic church goals.

4. New Church Development

New church development or church planting is one of the classic functions of church development. Referred to as church extension in some denominational traditions, it reflects the effort to extend denominational reach into new population centers. In more recent history, new church development can also encompass the initiation of new churches among the ever increasingly diverse racial/ethnic population of the United States. In many cases, these efforts, while new, may occur in neighborhoods and communities that have been populated for some time.

We look back in time first and then turn toward the future.

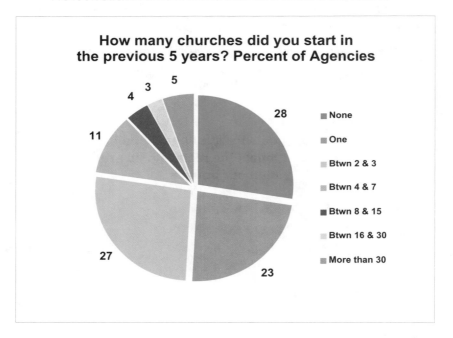

Number of New Church Starts During Past Five Years

The typical number of churches started over the last five years was one. According to the following chart, more than 27 percent of all represented governing bodies did not initiate any new churches in the past five years.

Denominationally, almost 54 percent of all Episcopal dioceses started no new churches compared to only 13 percent of Disciples regions. Inversely, 44 percent of Disciples regions started between two and three churches.

Targets for Starting New Congregations

Fifty-eight percent of the governing bodies indicated that they had a specific target for starting new churches over the next five years. In contrast, 32 percent did not have a specific target.

Again, there is diversity across the denominational groups. The

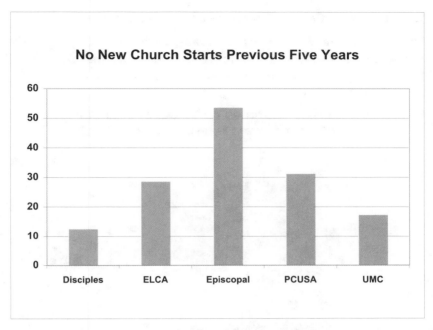

chart reveals that a greater percentage of Disciples, ELCA and United Methodist regional bodies have set specific church plant targets than have Presbyterians (PCUSA) or Episcopalians. Among the first three groups, 70 percent of their agencies had targets.

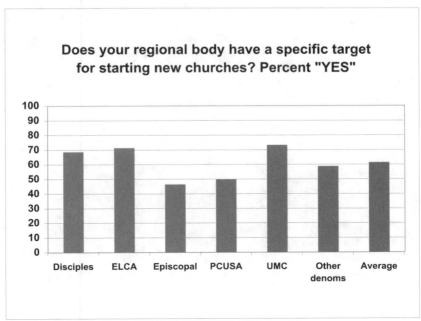

Number of New Church Targets over Next Five Years

Assuming a Regional Body has targets, how large is their vision? This next item looks at how many new church starts have been targeted over the next five years. The typical projected number of starts per regional body is three.

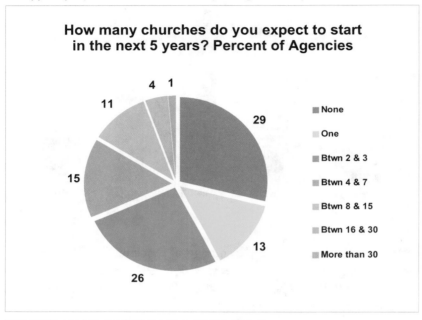

How many churches do you expect to start in the next 5 years? Percent of Agencies

- None
- One
- Btwn 2 & 3
- Btwn 4 & 7
- Btwn 8 & 15
- Btwn 16 & 30
- More than 30

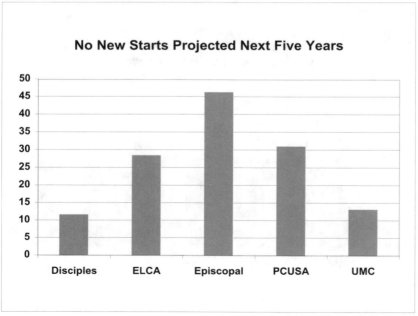

No New Starts Projected Next Five Years

Twenty-nine percent of all governing bodies represented in the survey do not expect to start a single new church. Thirteen percent expect to start only one over five years. Together, 42 percent of these governing bodies project as of the survey that they will plant one or less churches. (One wonders how these denominations' national goals are supposed to be met.)

How does this look by denomination?

Forty-six percent of all Episcopal dioceses represented in the survey do not project starting a single church. This is also true for nearly a third of all Presbyterian Church (USA) presbyteries. Lutheran (ELCA) synods are not far behind with 29 percent indicating no new start targets.

Models

New churches generally are built upon some kind of conceptual model and that model becomes the primary approach for development. There will, of course, be overlap among the various models, but it is the dominant factor that drives the approach that determines the model. We discerned seven models and one non-model.

Pastor-Developer/Church Planter

Twenty-three percent were built on the Pastor-Developer or Church Planter model. This model revolves around a key person sent to start a congregation.

Congregation Initiated

Eleven percent followed the congregation-initiated model. In this model, the initiative begins with a local congregation (sometimes more than one).

Regional Body Project

Nearly 29 percent were developed using the regional body project model. A new church originates as a work of the regional body.

Cooperative

The Cooperative Model is some combination of all or portions of the first three. Just over 14 percent were started following this approach.

Nesting

This model refers to the practice of starting a racial/ethnic ministry on the campus of an existing church but as a separate entity. This only represented 2 percent of the starts.

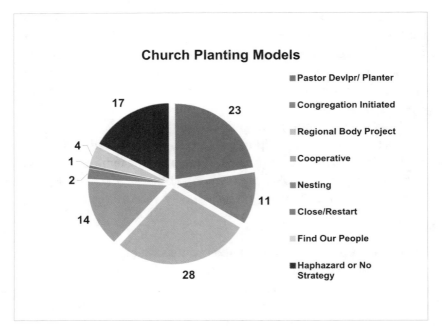

Church Planting Models

17　23
4
1
2
11
14
28

- Pastor Devlpr/ Planter
- Congregation Initiated
- Regional Body Project
- Cooperative
- Nesting
- Close/Restart
- Find Our People
- Haphazard or No Strategy

Close/Restart

Normally this model would be classified as part of a redevelopment strategy but was listed as a model by several respondents.[2]

Find Our People/Extend the Franchise

We were a bit surprised to find this model still pursued but 4 percent start a new church based upon the "Find Our People/Extend the Franchise" approach. This model emphasizes looking for areas where a denominational tradition does not have a church and where there is a high likelihood that people who prefer that tradition live.

Haphazard-No Strategy

This really is not a model, but several respondents indicated that their model was haphazard, or that they did not have a model. Favorite line: "What strategy?" Amazingly, over 17 percent indicated this was their approach.

5. Redevelopment

The fifth category of the findings looks at how redevelopment is done. Just over one in three regional agencies has set goals for addressing redevelopment church needs.[3] Forty-four percent indicated that they

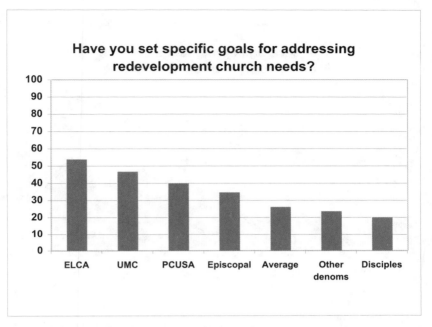

Have you set specific goals for addressing redevelopment church needs?

did not have goals and 20 percent did not know.

Again, there was a fair amount of diversity across the denominational traditions. More ELCA synods (54 percent) have set redevelopment goals than any other denominational tradition, followed by United Methodist conferences at 47 percent.

6. Challenges

The sixth category focuses on challenges church development leaders face. These were originally open-ended comments but through an analysis of them, five themes emerged. This is not the time to dig into them. Simply listing the theme areas and the percentage of comments that fell under each really tells the story.

The Themes Are: 1) Funding 2) Congregational Issues 3) Regional Issues 4) Leadership 5) Denominational Issues 6) Other—a catch all category.

The graph demonstrates again the recurrent theme of leadership. On average one in four comments dealt with some aspect of leadership. Surprisingly, funding came in lower than other challenges.

7. Staffing

One face of leadership for church development is professional staffing.

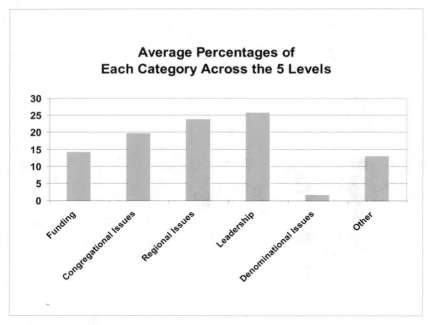

Executive Staff Responsible for Congregational Development

Three-fourths of all regional agencies surveyed do have an executive staff person directly responsible for church development. Of course, this also

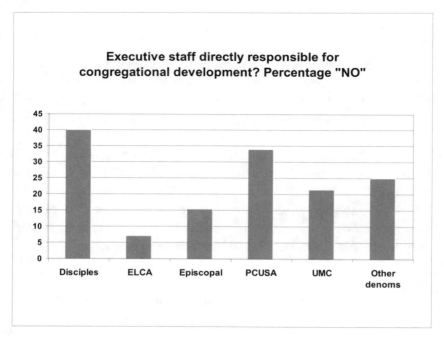

indicates that one in four do not.

Disciples and Presbyterians are the most likely not to allocate executives to church development.

Time Available for Congregational Development

Almost two out of three respondents do not believe that staff has enough time to devote to church development.

8. Preparing Leadership to Serve

The eighth category focuses on how different regional agencies prepare new members for their task of planning and coordinating church development activities. Respondents were invited to check all that apply.

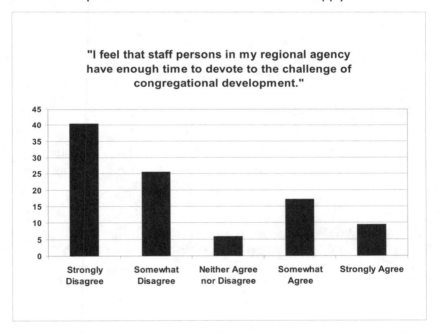

"I feel that staff persons in my regional agency have enough time to devote to the challenge of congregational development."

Not one of the options received even 50 percent. The chart provides the percentages marked "yes" for each of the eight options.

Almost half of the agencies provide committee members with documents as part of their approach to preparation. A third have some informal meetings designed to orient people.

Demographics have become a staple part of most church development planning and implementation processes. Almost 3 in 10 give training in the interpretation of demographics. Remember, by the way, that everyone who took the survey had a contract with Percept to provide them with

demographics. This means that less than a third of the Percept clients who obtain demographics actually train their people in what they have. Nearly one in four do not provide any kind of preparation, formal or informal.

The two most formal approaches to preparation, training events

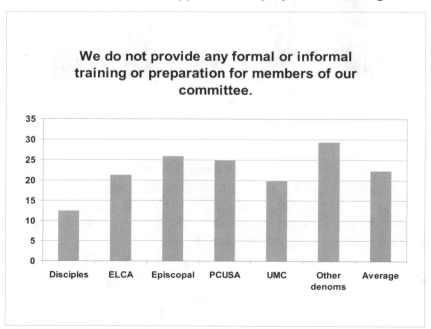

and/or team-building retreats are least practiced.

The denominational story across these is also interesting. I have chosen just two to illustrate. The two represent the extremes of providing formal training and not providing any training.

First of all, nobody exceeds 33 percent. That means that 66 percent do not provide formal training. Beyond that, only the United Methodists exceed 20 percent with both the Lutherans (ELCA) and the Episcopalians at less than 10 percent. Conversely, many provide absolutely no preparation.

One must ask whether we are really doing an adequate job of preparing people for this important work.

9. Financial Support

The final category is financial support. Budget allocations reflect agency priorities. As the chart shows, a third of all agencies represented in the survey allocate less than 10 percent to church development. After this, percentage allocations drop dramatically. We are not quite certain of what to think about nearly 30 percent having no idea how much gets allocated.

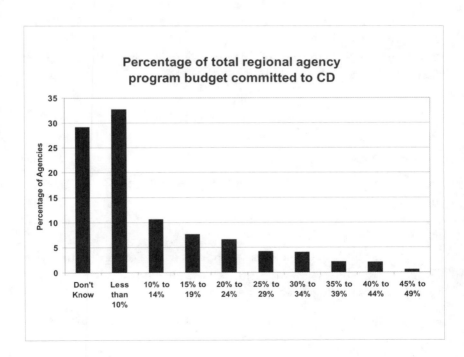

Two General Conclusions

These nine categories provide insight into the current state and practice of church development. It is possible to draw a couple of general conclusions. First of all, leadership was a constant issue. There is concern for recruitment. There is concern for adequate capability of leaders. There is concern in some cases that leadership is not properly trained or prepared for the task. And, in our estimate, a factor contributing to the leadership issue is the approach to leader preparation.

A second general finding suggests that some denominational systems are doing better than others are. A correlative to this, we believe is the size of the regional body. Some of the denominational traditions that consistently had the most struggles in the data also tended to have the smallest regional bodies. The best case in point is the Presbyterians. The size of the regional body seems to affect how well they can organize and implement their effort.

Conclusion

With this information, we have a pretty good picture of the current state of church development and how it is practiced. But this is only the first part of our search. In the next chapter, we will unveil the 10 Best Practices discovered through the analysis of the survey data.

Engagement Guide

The Purpose

To discuss the survey findings and practices and relate them to your regional body.

Group Discussion Questions

This chapter provided the general findings from Percept's Survey of Congregational Development Practices. Discuss first your overall impressions using the following questions.

- *What did you find the most surprising? Why were you surprised?*

- *What did you find the most disturbing? Discuss the reasons for your concern? Could you relate in some way to the findings? How so?*

- *What did you find the most encouraging? Discuss the reasons for your encouragement? Could you relate in some way to the findings? How so?*

- *How do you think your regional body compares to some of the findings?*

More specifically, discuss the following:

- *What is the level of commitment in your regional body to church development? Is it growing, stable or declining?*

- *Does your regional body have a strategic plan to guide your efforts in church development? If not, why?*

- *Discuss your regional body's leadership capacity. Do you have adequate professional staffing?*

- *How do you prepare people to serve?*

- *Based upon this chapter and discussion, what is the most important learning for you?(Have each person present answer this question.)*

ENDNOTES

[1] Claire Burkat, Roy Oswald, Transformational Regional Bodies: Promote Congregational Health, Vitality and Growth (Life Structure Resources, 2001)

[2] There were two types. The first type closed an existing church and re-opened as a new congregation, usually better reflecting racial/ethnic configuration of the surrounding community. The second type also "closed" the existing congregation but restarted over, with some of the members of the prior congregation but with a new mission emphasis. Less than one percent are developed using this approach.

[3] NOTE: We admit to an apparent bias in the survey design. Percept was unaware of how few of its client agencies did not use the term redevelopment to describe these efforts. While it has been the term we use in most client interactions, we have to wonder if we are communicating well around these themes given the way fact that so few outside the Presbyterians (PCUSA) and Lutherans (ELCA) use the term. This also suggests, unfortunately, that some of the survey questions are biased against those unfamiliar with the term. We deeply regret this but are also glad for the learning.

5

The 10 Best Practices:
THE DISCOVERIES

José **sat at his desk**, staring at the wall. He had just been installed in his Diocese as the new Canon for Congregational Development. It was a new position for the Diocese. There had not been a staff person directly responsible for the task of working with congregations and starting new ones for 40 years. Since that time, only one new congregation had been formed. The hiring of José represented a new era in the life of the Diocese. That was the good news, and José knew it. But as he sat at his desk, he was also aware of the bad news. With no history and no traditions, what was he supposed to do? Where did he start? How should the Diocese structure itself for this new commitment? He knew he would be given some time to get his feet underneath him, but not forever. It would be really helpful if there were a list of essential practices that had been demonstrated to be effective in facilitating and giving clear focus to a regional body's church development effort.[1]

In the previous chapter, we have looked at the current state and practice of church development based upon Percept's Congregational Development survey. But as stated in the previous chapter, our real hope and goal was to discern in the data a set of practices that is true wherever there is a robust effort. We now turn our concentration to this question.

To get at this, we subjected the data to statistical correlation analysis. Correlation analysis looks for variables that move together or against each other. If Variable A increases and Variable B does as well in a similar fashion, they are considered to be positively correlated. If Variable A moves in one direction and Variable C moves in the opposite direction relative to A, then it is considered negatively correlated. Non-correlated variables do not move in any pattern that is statistically related. Such correlations do not imply causality, though there may be a causal relationship. We can say, however, that clearly where either a positive or a negative correlation occurs, the two variables are influencing each other. Thus if A moves up,

B will as well. For example, a survey asks A) Do you like hamburgers? and B) Do you like French fries? Analysis showed that people who liked hamburgers were likely to like French fries as well. Conversely, those who did not like hamburgers did not like French fries. The two questions are positively correlated. Thus, it is reasonable to assume that where one is true, the other will be as well.

The Discovery

Using correlation analysis, we made an important discovery, a discovery that became our working hypothesis. We found that where there was a commitment to church development in a regional body, there also tended to be other activities and practices that suggested some level of a positive effort. Conversely, where there was not a commitment, it was more likely that efforts were anemic.

While the most important factor was commitment, two other variables seemed to track closely with it 1) a commitment that was growing and 2) the articulation of a strategic plan to guide church development. We found that where there was a growing commitment and a strategic plan, which translated that commitment into a roadmap, things were happening. Where these were missing, things were less likely to be happening.

Using this as our operating hypothesis, the regional agencies represented in the survey were segmented into three types. There were those who matched the description, those that did not match it at all and those who fell somewhere in the middle. Each group was given a descriptive name: "The Focused," "The Unfocused" and "The Distracted."

Three Types

The Focused

The Focused made up 29 percent of all regional bodies. This type bore two characteristics overall and several that supported them. The first characteristic was a strong commitment as a regional body to church development. The second characteristic was the articulation, adoption and implementation of a strategic plan for church development, which was perceived as a main reason for the growing commitment.

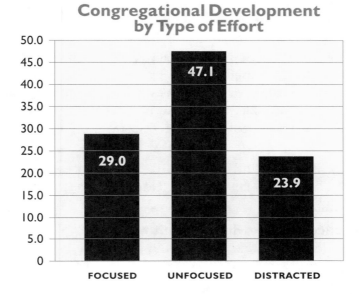

Congregational Development by Type of Effort

The Unfocused

The Unfocused at 47 percent was the largest type. Generally, they had a somewhat high commitment to church development. However, either the commitment was less likely to be growing or they were not as likely to have adopted and implemented a strategic plan.

The Distracted

The Distracted comprised 24 percent of the regional bodies. They neither had a commitment or a strategic plan. As a result, other elements that would be true about the focused often were not true for the distracted. While the first was Focused, the Distracted were sidetracked by both 1) a lack of focus on church development and 2) other issues that diverted their attention.

The State of Church Development

We can now come back full circle and add another dimension to our statement about the state of church development in the U.S. It ranges from very distracted to very focused. Where focused, there is evidence of accomplishment. Where distracted, there is less evidence of accomplishment and more frustration and uncertainty.

The next step in our analysis was to understand better what was true about the Focused group. Again, correlation analysis was applied and we noted the variables that positively correlated with a growing commitment. The Best practices are based upon what we found to be true about those regional bodies that fit the "Focused" type. The data demonstrate that the Focused share certain practices in common that are not as true for the Unfocused or the Distracted. Our analysis found 10 Practices that were true to varying degrees. It is our contention a robust effort will be demonstrable where these 10 Practices are in evidence. Where these are not evident to some considerable degree, the effort will be weak.

The 10 Practices

Best Practice #1: Growing Commitment
A growing commitment to congregational development at the regional level

The first and most important best practice focuses on the level of commitment to church development. It makes sense logically.

A robust church development effort will be founded upon a strong commitment that is growing. Where commitment was lacking or weak, so also was evidence of consistent accomplishments. Evidence of this commitment is revealed in the remaining nine Best Practices.

A best practice will work toward building a growing commitment to church development throughout the regional agency.

Key Facts

- *100% of the Focused indicated a strong level of commitment.*

- *0% of the Distracted indicated a strong level of commitment.*

- *96% of the Focused indicated that commitment had grown over the past two years.*

- *28% of the Distracted indicated that commitment had grown over the past two years.*

Commentary

All meaningful action flows out of a commitment. Conventional wisdom would affirm this principle and the survey findings did as well. The most positively correlated item on the survey was the one about commitment. Where commitment exists one finds an environment that is open to engaging the challenges presented by church development today. Where it does not exist, there is little heart to drive such an effort. It is also important, we found, that the commitment needed to be growing. The data would suggest that commitment begets more focused action which begets further commitment. The opposite scenario is also true.

But commitment is not enough. The Unfocused also declare a pretty high commitment level but many of the remaining practices do not exist. Commitment must translate into the rest of the Best Practices.

Best Practice #2: Strategic Plan

An adopted strategic plan for church development that provides overall vision and direction

Coupled with commitment was a strategic plan. Most Focused agencies have established a strategic plan for church development. The strategic plan shapes their vision and guides their efforts. In fact, what keeps an Unfocused from being a Focused is the lack of a strategic plan. A strategic plan will include a clear statement of the agency's vision for church development, its organizational mission and values and a statement of strategic initiatives to guide efforts over a three- to five-year period of time.

A best practice will ensure that a strategic plan for church development is created, adopted and implemented.

Key Facts

- *100% of the Focused indicated that a reason for the growth of commitment to church development was the articulation and adoption of a strategic plan.*

- *43% of the Focused have a set schedule for both strategic and annual planning and budgeting based upon extensive environmental analysis. Only 15% of the Distracted have such a set schedule.*

- *Nearly 80% of the Focused indicated they have established a strategic plan for church development. 85% of the Distracted indicated they HAD NOT established such a plan.*

Commentary

A good plan is the first step in translating commitment into an actual effort. We have also noticed that where a plan does not exist, an agency has no direction. It knows it needs to do something, but what? A strategic plan is essential to giving commitment shape, form and direction. Without a plan, commitment will dissipate quickly.

Best Practice #3: Specific Targets

Specific targets or goals set for new church development, redevelopment and racial/ethnic development

To further clarify the strategic plan, Focused agencies set specific targets or goals for new church development, redevelopment and racial/ethnic church development. These may be part of the plan, nested under one or more strategic initiatives, or they may stand on their own. To be a best practice, however, they must be based upon and stay tied to the strategic plan.

A best practice will set specific targets or goals for new church development, redevelopment and racial/ethnic church development that is tied to the larger strategic plan for church development.

Key Facts

- *85% of the Focused had new church development targets while only 36% of the Distracted did.*

- *68% of the Focused set goals for addressing the needs of congregations experiencing community or congregation-wide changes. Only 21% of the Distracted had such goals.*

- *55% of the Focused set goals for church development that reflect the racial/ethnic profile within their bounds while only 15% of the Distracted set such goals.*

- *60% of all the Focused set specific redevelopment goals. Only 21% of the Distracted set such goals.*

Commentary

Over the years, we have noticed that many church organizations set targets. This happens at the national level as well as the regional level. But these targets may not have any correlation to an environmental analysis or organizational capability. We have often wondered where the numbers come from. Our suspicion is that they are made up based upon some clever correlation with a date or event—for example, 200 by 2000. Two-hundred new churches by 2000 seems like a wonderful target. But upon what is it based other than its clever connection to the year 2000? This kind of specific goal setting is not helpful. For targets to be meaningful and an expression of a best practice, they must be tied to something larger and strategic, such as a strategic plan (see practice

#2) that is based upon strategic information (see practice #7).

Do national goals or targets serve this purpose? The survey indicated that many denominations set national goals for church development. But we found that there was no positive statistical correlation between such goals and what made a regional agency a Focused one. The positive correlation was to a regional strategic plan that included specific targets.

Best Practice #4: Measurable Action
Evidence of focused action toward meeting goals

At the end of the day, it is accomplishments that are the measure of a robust effort. Commitment and plans are critical and foundational. But they must translate into real accomplishments. It is not enough to have a strategic plan and specific targets. Focused agencies evidence measurable action toward meeting the goals or hitting the targets. New church or racial/ethnic church targets are established and actions to meet them set in motion. The evidence is in the fact of new churches or ministries being started. Where this occurs, there is an accomplishment that can be measured.

A best practice is the actual completion of goals or meeting of targets in a measurable way.

Key Facts

- *36% of the Focused started more than three churches in the prior five years compared to 3% for the Distracted.*

- *41% of the Distracted started no new churches in the prior five years compared to 30% of the Focused.*

- *46% of the Distracted started no Racial/Ethnic initiatives in the prior five years compared to only 21% of the Focused.*

- *81% of the Focused expect to close more churches in the next five years whereas only 62% of the Distracted do.*

Commentary

The kind of action envisioned in this practice is not the reactive kind. All three types, Distracted, Unfocused and Focused closed churches in the prior five year period at similar percentage levels. But this was different than more proactive types of activities such as new church development and racial/ethnic ministry development. Our suspicion is that closing churches may reflect a response to reality—churches are failing regardless of whether the agency involved is Distracted or Focused. But to start new churches of any kind or put in motion strategies to assist churches in changing situations takes a more proactive approach.

Can church closing be a proactive strategy? Well, certainly nobody wants to see a church close. But a proactive approach looks forward and anticipates where such may be required and plans and puts in place strategies accordingly. The Distracted are less likely to do this than the Focused. While the percentage of Distracted and Focused who closed churches in the previous five years were similar, the Focused were far more likely to expect to close more in the future.

Best Practice #5: Integrated Planning

Annual plan evaluation, goal-setting and budgeting are integrated into the rhythm of the regional agency

Annual planning is essential to any organization's effectiveness. Focused regional agencies have a clear understanding of annual planning and budgeting. There are three integrated steps. The first step is always an evaluation of prior year goal accomplishments and an assessment of the environment. The second is the process of annual goal setting based upon a) the larger strategic plan and b) the results of the evaluation process. The final step is setting budget priorities that are tied to the annual goals. Focused agencies have such a process built into their normal rhythm and each element of the process is included.

A best practice will adopt and implement an annual integrated planning process that includes, 1) evaluation, 2) goal setting and 3) budgeting tied to goals.

Key Facts

- *72% of the Focused develop goals annually; 43% tie these goals to their strategic plan. In contrast, 33% of the Distracted reduce annual planning to simply setting the budget. Some do not even do regional level planning.*

- *Twice as many of the Focused believe goal setting and annual budgeting are closely related as the Distracted.*

- *Two-thirds of the Focused set annual goals and tie them to budget allocations. Slightly more than a third of the Unfocused and Distracted follow this practice.*

Commentary

Annual planning, as outlined here, is essential to any organization's effectiveness. A strategic plan will lay out overall direction and create vision. But it is the annual planning and budgeting process that gives the strategic plan legs. Without a disciplined annual planning process, a strategic plan will sit on the shelf.

Best Practice #6: Capable Leadership

Experienced leadership capable of guiding congregational development efforts

Leadership was a consistent theme throughout many of the open-ended comments of the survey. When asked to identify the five greatest challenges of congregational development, the category of leadership represented one in four comments that focused on some aspect of leadership. Training, availability, problems with and lack of leadership abilities all emerged.

Among the Focused, a critical reason for the growth in commitment was the presence of leadership capacity to lead efforts forward. Conversely, the Distracted were more likely to suggest it was the lack of leadership that kept them from seeing commitment growth. When asked to indicate the most important consideration in filling congregational development committee positions, the Distracted ranked "Willingness to serve" first. The Focused, however, ranked "Experience in congregational development" as number one.

Experienced leadership capability is critical to a robust effort. As a best practice, efforts will be pursued to ensure that experienced leadership is available and allowed to guide.

Key Facts

- *Almost 80% of the Focused felt that leadership capacity was a reason for a growth in commitment to congregational development.*

- *41% of the Focused indicated that "experience in congregational development" was most important in filling committee positions. Only 23% of the Distracted felt experience was that important. Instead, 57% ranked "willingness to serve" as number one.*

- *While weak among all three types, 26% of the Focused provided formal training for new congregational development committee members. Only 10% of the Distracted followed this practice.*

Commentary

What sets the Focused apart from the rest of the types on the topic of Leadership? The research suggests it is the recognition that success is dependent upon leadership that knows what it is doing and is capable of doing it. It was a bit of a surprise to discover that the number-one reason for selecting committee members was finding people who were willing to sit on the committee. Such people may be faithful saints and willing servants, but they are not necessarily capable of leading. Yet capable leadership is critical to a robust effort.

Best Practice #7: Demographic Analysis

Vision for congregational development and ongoing planning are informed by regional demographic analysis

Church development deals with population dynamics. It identifies areas where new communities are taking shape and plans to plant a church. It monitors population profile changes in established areas. Changing neighborhoods impact existing congregations. New racial/ethnic groups move into communities providing new opportunities and challenges for church development. No matter where one looks, the task of church development must deal with demographic realities. Therefore, up-to-date demographic analysis is an essential tool for the robust effort. More fundamentally, however, is the need to found a regional vision on a clear understanding of the demographic dynamics occurring with an agency's bounds.

A best practice will ensure that demographic analysis tools are up-to-date and easily available to inform regional planning and decision-making.

Key Facts

- *Over 57% of the Focused felt that regional level demographic analysis provided the foundation for a new vision.*

- *92% of the Focused believed that providing demographic resources was an important activity of congregational development. At 85%, this practice actually ranked high for the Distracted as well.*

Commentary

While a large number of the Focused demonstrate this practice, the numbers are not as large as one would think. This is clearly an area of growth even for those who would be classified as Focused. Additionally, the fact that a) all of those who took the survey are clients of Percept (which means they have a license granting access to our demographic systems) and, b) that even the Distracted rank the value of demographics highly, it would seem that enhancing the use of what is already an available tool could only be positive.

Best Practice #8: Financial Support

A minimum allocation of 10 percent of the program budget for congregational development with a propensity to increase the percentage

Budget allocations reflect organizational values. Strategic plans that do not have money tied to them are doomed to fail. Focused agencies will allocate at least 10 percent of their program budget to church development. The Focused reflect a propensity to have that percentage increase. A financial support plan and significant budget allocations out of that plan are critical to successful church development efforts.

A best practice will insure that adequate (at least 10 percent of program budget) financial resources are available to fund plans.

Key Facts

- *55% of the Focused indicated that an increased financial commitment was a reason for the increased overall commitment to congregational development.*

- *45% of the Focused allocate 10% or more of the program budget while only 36% of the Distracted allocate this much. Nearly 37% of the Focused allocate more than 10% compared to only 20% of the Distracted.*

- *Of regional agencies with less than 75 churches, 73% of the Focused allocate 10% or more. This is compared to only 46% of the Distracted with less than 75 churches.*

- *55% of the Focused allocate $100,000 or more annually. Only 28% of the Distracted make such an allocation.*

Commentary

Analysis suggested that size is a significant factor, as one would expect. Smaller agencies (those with few churches) have less to work with, generally, than larger agencies. However, there were several agencies with under 75 churches that made aggressive allocations to support church development. The key learning was that everybody can do something if they want to, that is, if they make church development a priority.

This practice also raises a question about agency plans for building a capital fund to support the more expensive aspects of church development such as property purchases, building renovations, church planting, etc.

Best Practice #9: Designated Staff

At least one professional staff member for whom congregational development represents 50 percent or more of his/her portfolio

We have already seen that experienced leadership is essential to a robust church development effort. But having professional staff at the regional agency level that is focused on the effort is even more critical. Focused agencies will have at least one and often more than one professional staff member whose portfolio is at least 50 percent designated to church development. It is clear then that they allocate a significant amount of professional staff time to church development tasks and activities. The Distracted do not.

A best practice will insure that at least 50 percent of some executive staff member's time will be designated specifically to church development.

Key Facts

- *92% of all Focused designate executive staff directly responsible for congregational development. Less than 50% of the Distracted make such a designation.*

- *One in three of the Distracted have no staff designated for congregational development. In contrast, less than 9% of the Focused have no one.*

- *61% of the Focused have two or more executives designated compared to 15% of the Distracted.*

- *50% of the Distracted designate less that 25% of their professional staff time. In comparison, less than 30% of the Focused designate less than 25%.*

- *38% of the Focused designate more than 50% of their executive staff time to congregational development, with 22% exceeding 75% of their time.*

Commentary

Size of agency really did not matter much on this practice. Large or small, Focused agencies designated staff time to church development. Distracted agencies did not. We often hear from clients the frustration they feel because they simply do not have enough time to give to developing congregations. Nearly one in three of the Distracted agencies indicated that the reason that commitment declined was due to the fact that they have "too much overall regional body work with inadequate staff resources to allocate" to the task.

A question we often raise is this: What could be a more important task today than that of dealing with church development? If cultural factors are changing the way the demographics support that they are, then the challenges are mounting higher and higher. There is a point where the number of churches struggling within a region will become so high that the viability of the region itself is threatened. We believe that many agencies need to realign their priorities and express that realignment in a reallocation of professional staff time. Surely there are tasks that if left undone may make life a bit more untidy but will not threaten future viability. The same cannot be said for church development challenges.

Best Practice #10: Committee Preparation

An intentional process faithfully implemented to prepare congregational development committees

Most regional level efforts involve some kind of planning or coordinating committee. But to our surprise, the preparation of persons who join these committees is woefully inadequate. Not even the Focused do particularly well at this.

Respondents were given six different practices for preparing committee members. They ranged from giving them paper work and documents to formal training and team-building retreats. At best, the Focused gave new members documents and met informally with them. No one scored high on any of the more formal preparation processes. Most of the Distracted did not even give new members documents.

A best practice would design and implement a more formal preparation process for new and continuing church development committee members.

Key Facts

- *64% of the Focused provided new committee members with documents that outline current strategic plans, projects, policies and procedures that govern congregational development within their agency. Only 39% of the Distracted provided this minimal preparation.*

- *51% of the Focused at least held informal meetings with new members in contrast to only 21% of the Distracted.*

- *Only 38% of the Focused and 10% of the Distracted provided training in the interpretation of demographics, even though such training is readily available at no cost through Percept.*

> • *Only 21% of the Focused and 10% of the Distracted provided a formal training experience in preparation for their task and responsibility.*

Commentary

We believe this is a weakness across the board. How can we possibly expect a committee of people to meaningfully and effectively plan and coordinate efforts when they receive little, if any preparation? Even the Focused could grow significantly by giving more intentional attention to this practice. Formalized training for committee members must be designed and implemented.

Scorecard

Now two questions that might be in everyone's mind. First, having outlined the 10 Best Practices, how did the entire sample score? Maybe you asked this, maybe not. But I will bet many of you are thinking the second question: How did my denomination score relative to the others? I will conclude this portion on these two questions, making it brief but informative.

Scorecard for All Regional Bodies Together

In effect, creating a scorecard turns the 10 Best Practices into an evaluative tool. We are looking for the level of evidence of the practice in some group of regional bodies—or for each regional body present. Three possible levels were created: Minimal Evidence, Some Evidence or Considerable

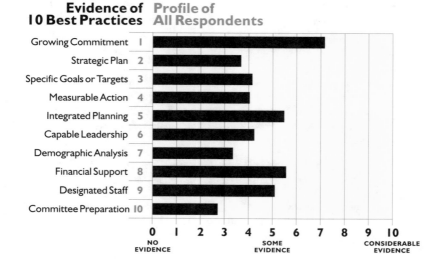

Evidence of 10 Best Practices   Profile of All Respondents

Growing Commitment	1
Strategic Plan	2
Specific Goals or Targets	3
Measurable Action	4
Integrated Planning	5
Capable Leadership	6
Demographic Analysis	7
Financial Support	8
Designated Staff	9
Committee Preparation	10

0 1 2 3 4 5 6 7 8 9 10
NO EVIDENCE   SOME EVIDENCE   CONSIDERABLE EVIDENCE

Evidence. These three were then translated into a single score between 0 and 10 with 10 representing the highest and one the lowest level of evidence.

The preceding graph shows in the aggregate where everyone falls.

The graph tells us that overall, everyone has a long way to go to demonstrate considerable evidence. As logical and somewhat self-evident as these 10 Practices are, the fact remains that they are not strongly evident in our regional bodies.

What would be helpful would be a view of this across an entire denomination. We, in fact, have this information for five of the denominations represented. Why only five? We needed to have a large enough sample set from enough agencies to develop a valid profile. We have such a profile for:

1. The United Methodists
2. The Presbyterian Church (USA)
3. The Evangelical Lutheran Church in America
4. The Episcopal Church
5. The Christian Church (Disciples of Christ)

A special report has been created for each of these denominations and is available to download online.

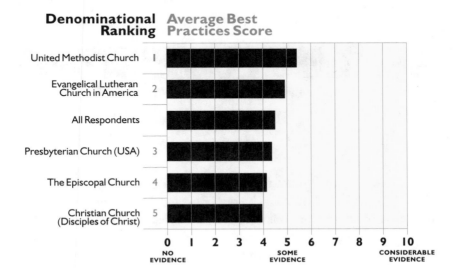

Denominational Ranking   Average Best Practices Score

United Methodist Church	1	
Evangelical Lutheran Church in America	2	
All Respondents		
Presbyterian Church (USA)	3	
The Episcopal Church	4	
Christian Church (Disciples of Christ)	5	

0   1   2   3   4   5   6   7   8   9   10

NO EVIDENCE   SOME EVIDENCE   CONSIDERABLE EVIDENCE

Scorecard Across the Denominations

Now the question of comparison. We have rolled up all 10 Best Practices into a single score for each of the denominational traditions with an adequate sample. We have then plotted the results in this next graph.

While nobody is setting the world on fire, the United Methodists at least break the score of five. Everyone else falls between four and five.

There is lots of work to do!

Conclusion

The last two chapters have focused on the question: What does it take to do an effective and successful job of developing congregations. We have discovered that regional bodies that are focused share certain common characteristics. The 10 Best Practices reflect these. The research would suggest that regional bodies that are likely to do an effective and successful job of developing congregations will have these practices evident to a large degree.

Additionally, with the articulation of the 10 Best Practices, we now have the full shape of our Vision for a Robust effort outlined. Chapter one raised three questions. We believe that solid answers to each of these will point us toward the elements of a robust church development effort. In fact, there is a specific element of the vision that speaks to each question, as demonstrated in the following table.

The Questions	The Element of a Robust Vision
Why do we care about the task?	A Passionate Faith
How do we think about the task?	Six Missiological Principles
How do we structure our regional bodies for the task?	10 Best Practices

Taken together, these three elements comprise a robust design for church development. It would be our hope, indeed, our dream, that you would begin to translate this vision into a robust reality in your regional bodies. This of course leads to an obvious next question. How do you realize this vision? That will be the focus of Part II of the book. Its emphasis is on "becoming the vision."

Engagement Guide

The Purpose

To discuss the 10 Best Practices and their applicability to your regional body.

Group Discussion Questions

Shift the discussion to the 10 Best Practices

- *What is your initial reaction to the 10 Best Practices? Give explanations.*

- *Were there any surprises?*

- *Based upon your initial encounter with the 10 Best Practices, what do you perceive to be the level of evidence of the Best Practices in your regional body?*

- *Are there particular practices that are more evident in your regional body? Less evident?*

- *Can you imagine introducing and integrating these practices into your regional body?*

- *Do you think there would be obstacles? If so, what do you think they would be? What could you do to address the obstacles?*

- *What do you intend to do with the 10 Best Practices?*

With the conclusion of this chapter, the shape of the vision for a robust church development effort has been fully outlined. Spend a few minutes discussing the overall vision.

- *What were the three elements? What were the three questions asked that each element addressed?*

- *Can you imagine beginning to translate this vision into reality in your regional body? Discuss pros and cons of doing so.*

ENDNOTES

[1] The story of José is really a composite of several regional bodies. It accurately represents a problem that exists, though the story itself has been compiled from several stories in order to not focus on a particular situation and in order to emphasize the problem of knowing how to structure for congregational development.

6

Prepare to Realize

Everyone has dreams. Most people from time to time imagine themselves doing something different, living somewhere different or being someone different. But not everyone is successful at transforming those dreams into living reality. For many the dreams are no more than wishful thinking. But some people's dreams become more than wishful thinking, they become captivating visions that they make real. Such people are true leaders.

In Part I we focused on the shape of a vision for church development. But at this point, as filled out as that vision is, there is no guarantee that it is more than wishful thinking. The true test of whether it is a captivating vision or just wishful thinking is in what you do with the vision. Therefore, the primary question for Part II is this: How do you turn this vision into reality in your setting? How do you become the vision? Or, how do you realize the vision in your regional body? How might you go about making the dream real?

This is quite a challenge and one that needs careful consideration. The focus of the next two chapters is the challenge of realizing the vision. That is, turning the vision into reality in your regional body. How do you do that? We will consider three questions whose answers will assist you to realize the vision. The three questions are:

1. *How do you prepare yourself to realize the vision?*

2. *How do you help people process the need to realize the vision?*

3. *How do you develop a plan for realizing the vision?*

To address these, you must prepare, you must process and you must plan if you hope to see the vision realized in your regional body. In this chapter, we will look at the question of preparation. What will it take from you as a leader? And what tools and processes will you need to assist you? In the subsequent chapter we will propose an outline for helping people process the need to realize the vision and for developing a plan to realize the vision. The Engagement Process for Chapter Seven provides outlines for two leadership development retreats.

Preparing to Realize

How do you prepare yourself to realize the vision? It is important that you be clear about the challenge represented in this vision and what it will take to realize it. The challenge is about change. Based upon the data and what we discovered about how the different denominational traditions are succeeding, there is room for significant growth across all traditions. This growth will require change. You are aware of the need for change. It is bantered about so much you would have to be living in complete isolation to have missed all the rhetoric calling us to change. Ultimately, your challenge is to lead change. To do so, you must prepare yourself if you hope to realize this vision.

I believe there are three things you will need to do in preparation to realize the vision:

> 1) Develop a proper personal perspective on what the challenge will demand of you.
>
> 2) Size the challenge. How big is it?
>
> 3) Acquire the tools you will need in order to meet the challenge.

Preparing Yourself

How do you prepare yourself? Perspective is critical. You must first recognize what the challenges will require of you. Think of someone that you know who has successfully led a change effort. How would you characterize that person? What was it about this leader that seemed to carry him or her through the process? Stop reading for a moment and reflect on this person. Write down a list of characteristics that you recall about this leader.

Although one could think of many personal characteristics of change leaders, three are critical and are necessary if you would be prepared to meet the challenge of leading change. When I read about the life of Dr. Martin Luther King, Jr., I see each of these.

1. Commitment. The first thing you need to prepare yourself for the challenge is a commitment to realize the vision yourself. We will discuss this more fully in the next chapter, but it begins here. Leaders must lead and to lead means making a commitment to a vision and then passionately working to realize it. If you are half-hearted about the task, the results will be also. You must believe that the vision is right and that it must be realized.

When I think of a person who has successfully led a change effort, Reverend Jill Hudson, Executive Presbyter of the Presbytery of Whitewater Valley comes to mind. Jill realized that if her presbytery was to continue to effectively serve its churches and do church development, it must change its ethos and ways of doing things. Jill also knew that if this was going to occur, then she, as the executive needed to fully commit to the process. She could not be half-hearted about it. She could not have one foot in the water and the other on the shore, always sensing the direction of opinion. She had to be fully committed to the goal and then lead from that place.

2. Patience. *With commitment comes a need for patience. Change is tough, even when the need for it is obvious. Part of preparing yourself is accepting the need to be patient and long-suffering. Change takes time, and people need space to grow. But patience is not passivity. Sometimes I think we confuse the two words. Patience is a virtue. Passivity is not. I fear we have too many people in leadership positions in the church who outwardly seem like patient souls but who are really just disengaged. Patience gives people space but still urges them to move forward with you.*

Jill Hudson epitomizes the patient, not passive, leader. She was very clear with her leadership about what needed to be done. And she prodded where appropriate. But she also gave people space to grow into the new vision for her presbytery.

Dr. King promoted and practiced non-violence. But he was not passive. He was a patient man, but he was not passive. He gave people space. But he would not let things stand still. To lead change, you must be patient but you must also insist that your regional body move forward.

3. Focus. *Moving forward requires a clear focus as well as commitment and patience. Change leaders "keep their eye on the ball." Distractions are everywhere. I have several friends who are regional level staff. It seems that too much of their life is about putting out today's fires. The distractions are constant. Having a clear vision for church development helps. The clearer the vision, the easier to keep focused. But keeping focused still requires effort. Leaders keep their focus amidst all of the noise that will forever surround them.*

Jill never lost her focus. The changes she was trying to accomplish took several years. And her presbytery went through some extremely difficult and heart-wrenching events. But she never lost her focus and the fruit is evident today in how her presbytery functions.

If Dr. King was anything, he was focused. There were distractions all around him, all the time. Some of the distractions were petty. Some were dangerous. But he kept his focus and kept the movement focused. Change requires a leader who knows where she or he is going and keeps the focus forever on that goal.

The first part of preparation is recognizing what the effort will require of you. You must be committed, patient and focused if you would lead in the realization of the Robust Vision.

Sizing the Challenge

The second part of preparation is sizing the challenge. How big is it? What is the scope? In my estimation, there are two pieces to the challenge. The most obvious challenge is knowing what to do and how to do it to. While lack of vision will lead you nowhere, too many so-called visionaries do not know how to translate a vision into a functional reality. Knowing what will be required and a process for accomplishing it is part of sizing the challenge.

But there is a greater challenge and it has the greatest potential to sidetrack the effort. Simply put, it is the challenge of dealing with attitudes that sabotage attempts at change. You may know what to do and how to do it but unless people's attitudes are able and willing to embrace the vision, change efforts will fail.

What do I mean by an attitude? Most of us recognize that attitudes reflect a complex of feelings, life experiences, beliefs and values that influence our mindset or outlook on life. For some folks, change raises suspicious attitudes. Possibly rooted in fear or "turf control" or a host of other factors, such attitudes can easily neutralize attempts to move something forward. We have all seen such blocking behaviors in our churches. They are evident at regional levels as well. It does little good to simply complain about this. It is reality. So, we must assess the size of the attitude challenge to be faced. What are the prevailing attitudes among those responsible for church development in your regional body? Are your fellow leaders open, are they tentative or do they block change efforts? Knowing the attitude challenge is part of sizing the overall challenge you face in leading change efforts.

Tools in Preparation

To meet these two challenges, you need tools. There are two kinds of tools needed. The first are knowledge tools and the second, process tools.

Knowledge Tools

Relevant knowledge and understanding is critical if a change in attitude and ultimately in practice is to occur. You must know at least three things; 1) the Vision of a Robust Effort in its three elements, 2) the current status of your regional body relative to the vision and 3) the current attitudes of your leaders toward changing how you conduct church development. Let's consider each of these in more detail:

> *1. The Three Elements: First, you must have a clear understanding of the three elements of a Robust Church development Effort. You must be clear about the shape of the vision. You must understand the important role passionate faith plays in a robust effort. You must know and understand the missiological principles that provide the conceptual framework for your work. And you must see in the 10 Best Practices a model for structuring your efforts. The whole purpose of Part I of this book is to unpack that vision and using the Engagement Discussions, lead others in that same reflection.*

> *2. Current Status: Second, you must know the current status of the regional body relative to the Vision. In other words, how does your regional body measure up relative to the vision? This is not for judgment purposes. It is for assessment purposes. The vision tells you where you want to be, but you also must know where you are if you are to plot a meaningful course toward the vision. You assess where you are so you can compare that to where you want to go. Assessment is a diagnosis that allows you to know what to prescribe as a regimen of change.*

But how do you do that? Ideally, there would be an assessment instrument tied in some way to the three elements of a robust effort, allowing an "apples to apples" comparison. There is such an instrument for those who are Percept VISTA clients! It can be found on Percept's VISTA2000 web site. It is called "A Measure or Robustness." Its goal is to provide you a measure of the robustness of your church development effort.

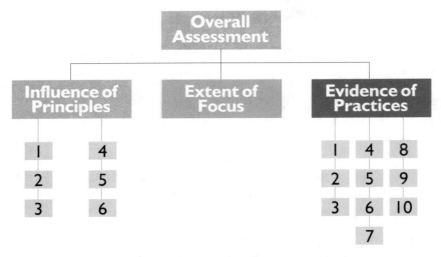

Assessment Tool: A Measure of Robustness

What does it measure? The survey measures three things. First, it looks at the level of Influence the Six Missiological Principles have in how a regional body does church development.

Second, it assesses the Extent of Focus within a regional body and compares that to the national average derived from our national survey. Extent of Focus is based upon two things; a growing commitment and the presence of a strategic plan for church development.

Third, it assesses the level of evidence of each of the 10 Best Practices within the regional body and again compares these to the national averages.

What does the report look like? There are two parts to the report. Part I is the Assessment Section. In this section, the scores for the regional body are given. All scoring is on a 0 to 10 scale with 10 being good. Each item assessed includes both a numeric score and a text summary of its meaning. Part II is called Recommendations. This section provides narrative recommendations for actions that are derived from the scores in Part I.

There are three levels of detail in the Assessment portion of the report. It begins at a high level of generalization and then becomes more specific.

1. Overall Assessment. A composite score of all three areas is assessed—namely, the Influence of the Missiological Principles, the Extent of Focus and the Evidence of the Best Practices. Note in the illustration below the score is 3.3 out of a total possible of 10. The textual summary translates that to Somewhat Weak. Interpreted, that means given the score across the entire survey, this regional body's measure of robustness is "somewhat weak." Other options are "Very weak," "Somewhat Strong" or "Very Strong" Of course the hope would be a "Very Strong" score.

OVERALL ASSESSMENT OF ROBUSTNESS	SCORE
Somewhat Weak	**3.3**

AGGREGATE ASSESSMENT	SCORE	RESULT
Influence of Principles	3.8	Minimal Influence
Extent of Focus	2.5	Distracted
Evidence of Practices	3.5	Minimal

2. Aggregate Assessment. *All three areas of assessment are rolled up and a score for each presented. Note the three areas. They are 1) Influence of the Principles, 2) Extent of Focus and 3) Evidence of the Practices. It is the averaging of these three scores that provides the Overall Assessment score. But this level allows you to see across the three areas more specifically where one is strong or weak.*

In our illustration, the Influence of the Principles score indicates minimal influence with a score of 3.8 out of 10. Weak though this score is, it is still the best score. The Extent of Focus drops to 2.5. The text indicates it is in the distracted zone. Finally, the Evidence of the Practices rises a little to 3.5 but it still gets an interpretation of Minimal Evidence.

3. Detailed Assessment. *Actual scores are presented for each of the three areas. This is the greatest level of detail and therefore pinpoints where the real weak spots are, or conversely, where the really strong points are.*

Influence of the Missiological Principles

In the example report on the following page, note that some of the Missiological Principles are more influential than some others. The principle that God is a missionary God has Significant Influence, but the idea that Mission in North America is a cross-cultural enterprise has No Influence over how this regional body conducts church development.

INFLUENCE OF MISSIOLOGICAL PRINCIPLES	SCORES	RESULT
1) God is a missionary God	8	Significant Influence
2) God calls us to participate in that mission as God's people, the church	2	Minimal Influence
3) Mission in N. America is a cross-cultural missionary enterprise	0	No Influence
4) Contextual analysis is critical to effective engagement	6	Some Influence
5) It is the church's responsibility to translate	1	Minimal Influence
6) Missionary Leadership is required at each level of the church	6	Some Influence

Extent of Focus

The Extent of Focus section simply restates the score in the Aggregate Assessment section but here it is compared with the national average. Note that with a score of 2.5, it is below the National Average of 4.3.

EXTENT OF FOCUS ON CONGREGATIONAL DEVELOPMENT	SCORES	RESULT
National Average	4.3	Unfocused
Score	2.5	Distracted

Evidence of Best Practices

Finally, looking at the Evidence of Best Practices, we see that there is little real strength across any of the Practices (The red bars are National Averages). About the best it gets is Considerable Evidence in Practice #5, Integrated Planning. Only in two practices do they exceed the National Average. On every other Practice, they are below the National Average, in some cases, way below. Note specifically a score of "0" indicating "No Evidence" of Capable Leadership or Demographic Analysis.

EVIDENCE OF 10 BEST PRACTICES	SCORES		RESULT
1) Growing Commitment	7.1	6.0	Moderate Evidence
2) A Strategic Plan	3.7	3.3	Minimal Evidence
3) Specific Goals or Targets	4.1	6.7	Moderate Evidence
4) Measurable Action	4.0	1.7	Minimal Evidence
5) Integrated Planning	5.4	8.0	Considerable Evidence
6) Capable Leadership	4.2	0.0	No Evidence
7) Demographic Analysis	3.3	0.0	No Evidence
8) Financial Support	5.5	4.0	Moderate Evidence
9) Designated Staff	5.1	4.0	Moderate Evidence
10) Committee Preparation	2.8	1.4	Minimal Evidence

Part II of the Report provides the Recommendations. The Recommendations follow the same three-fold structure at the detail level. The idea of the Recommendations is to provide a way to engage the results. So, note that the example regional body, as we already noted, showed Minimal Evidence of the Missiological Principles. The Recommendation text then points them toward resources that will focus on these principles.

In like manner, the effort is Distracted, so the recommendation identifies specifically what must be addressed to increase their focus.

Part II: Recommendations

If our regional body is to focus on increasing the robustness of our effort, where should we concentrate?

Influence of Missiological Principles: MINIMAL

It would appear that your regional congregational development efforts are minimally (if at all) influenced by these missiological principles. It might prove helpful to begin an intentional conversation around them all. A good place to begin is in reading current literature on the subject. We have prepared a list of our Top Five books related to the church's mission in North America. (Click here) .

Congregational Development Effort: DISTRACTED

There are reasons why a regional agency is distracted. A good place to start is by asking questions. What are the things that capture most of your time or that of the region's leadership? Speak with other leaders about this. Try to clearly identify what is distracting your agency. Once the distractions have been identified, develop strategies for a) minimizing the ability of these issues to distract and b) raising the level of commitment to congregational development. Sometimes the distractions result from internal unresolved issues. If that is the case, you might consider engaging outside consultants trained in assisting organizations to process the conflicts. Percept can make recommendations. To send an email to one of the Client Support Coordinators, click here.

Recommendations for the 10 Best Practices are only provided when a score falls below the "Considerable Evidence" level. Recommendations typically ask questions or point toward helpful resources, or in some cases make suggestions for action.

Best Practice RECOMMENDATIONS FOR ACTION

Practice #1: Please refer to the recommendation outlined under the Congregational Effort section above. Those issues must be addressed before work on the rest of the 10 Practices will prove effective.

Practice #2: A key to a focused effort is a strategic plan for congregational development. It is important that one be developed. There are a couple of ways to accomplish this. The approach to take should consider the availability of capable and energetic leadership. (See scores for Practices #6 and #10) If you have strong enough leadership, Percept's VISTAPlan process is designed to guide a regional agency in the formulation of such a plan. It assumes a certain degree of self-direction with a consultant from Percept available as an option. If you do not have the internal leadership strength for such a process, you may need to engage an outside consulting group that specializes in assisting in the development of strategic plans. Percept can make recommendations. Contact your Client Support Coordinator. To send an email to one of the Client Support Coordinators, click here.

Practice #3: Many plans fail because they are too general. They lay out the broad strokes but fail to translate those into specific targets. If you have not set targets, what are the reasons? Some reasons include: 1. Did not really force the planning to be that specific. 2. Resistance to specific targets within the regional agency. 3. Fear of failure if targets are set and not met. There may be others. It is a good exercise to figure the barriers to setting clear and focused targets. In response, purpose now to set targets. Root those targets in the demography you receive from Percept and your strategic plan. Be aggressive but realistic. Set targets that stretch your regional body. Then go for them!.

Who Should Take the Survey?

A very important question is this: Who should take the survey? The way the survey is designed, it has tremendous flexibility. It is no longer primarily a research survey, it is an assessment tool. Additionally, it is intended to reflect the perception of the person taking it. So, one of its uses is as an awareness builder. Anyone in the regional body could conceivably take it. More probably, you could have staff and committee members take the survey, print their results and then in a meeting, share your results with each other. There will be a diversity of perspective reflecting the different perceptions of the regional body. That information alone will be useful to the whole effort.

Can the survey be taken more than once? Yes, you can use it as an ongoing assessment tool to check progress toward the vision. This works as long as you do not try to make the tool something it is not. It is not a totally scientifically valid assessment. It is possible, having taken the survey, to figure out how to make the scores move. But remember it is not a test, it is a feedback instrument.

What Should You Do with It?

Let me ask you a question. What could you do with this kind of information for your regional body?

With the Assessment results, you have a fairly good picture of how your regional body measures up to two of the three elements of a robust effort. It does not assess Passionate Faith, for obvious reasons. That is a personal issue and may be a good pastoral conversation to have as part of the large discussion but it can not be assessed. However, these other areas can be assessed and, with the results in hand, you are ready to move to the next level of the process.

> *3. Leaders' Attitudes. Third, I believe you need to know where your other leaders are and their likely disposition toward change. Part of the reason Percept developed the iChange tool was to provide this kind of insight. It is an important knowledge tool. Have your leaders take it and use the discussion materials as preparation for the larger discussion. (The iChange survey can be found on the Link2Lead.com site.)*

We often hear how people score on the assessment softens them to larger change discussions. For example, people whose change type is characterized as "Blocking" or "Tentative" often do not perceive themselves as obstacles to change. Most do not want to subvert change. Indeed, they are often not even aware this is how they emotionally and behaviorally respond to change initiatives. We have found that simply having the output of the iChange survey provides them a context for personal change through a moment of self-discovery. Knowledge can be a powerful, liberating resource and tools that expand knowledge are a powerful lever for change.

We have found this true relative to our demographic resources. They reveal what is true about a neighborhood. But we have also found they are powerful in revealing what is not true about a neighborhood. Sometimes it is the second discovery that softens people to consider the missional implications of the first.

Process Tools

The first tools you need are knowledge tools. The second tools are process tools. Process tools provide a way to move a group from one place to another and create a product along the way. What kinds of processes are needed? There are really two. The first type of process assists in developing a more positive attitude toward the change. Such processes are intended to facilitate the formation of consensus. The second type will assist in the development of a plan for change.

Consensus-Building Process

First, the consensus-building or attitude-adjustment process. When I was in college, I was invited by the Governor of the State of Washington to serve on a special task force called Alternatives for Washington. It was in that experience that I learned policy and planning processes. But I also had my first exposure to consensus building experiences as well. There were 150 of us from across the state, from all walks of life, all ages and racial/ethnic groups. We had private citizens and politicians, college presidents, business leaders and three college students, of which I was one. I remember arriving for the first three-day retreat. The packet I was given opened with the schedule. There would be an introductory plenary session early afternoon followed by an "attitude-adjustment hour" beginning at five. Dinner would be at 6:30. What, I wondered, was an attitude-adjustment hour? I soon found out. To the undiscerning observer, it looked much like a cocktail hour. That was because drinks were flowing. But looking more closely, one would also see that this time of informal exchange around drinks facilitated relationships, softening people toward one another and ultimately building trust. And trust would be essential if we were to accomplish the task the governor had given us. In the end, we needed to build consensus for a holistic vision for the state of Washington. But you do not build consensus with people you do not know and/or do not trust. The wheat farmer from eastern Washington did not automatically trust the urbane city politician.

Before you can build a plan with change initiatives, you must provide people with an attitude adjustment process that accomplishes similar objectives. If you want people to embrace the vision discussed in this book, you need a process that allows them to work through the implications of such a vision. It must be a process that liberates people to deal with the implications of the change that would be called for. It must be a process that helps people see more clearly all angles on the issue. And it must be a process that facilitates trust, for the success of a change effort is directly tied to trust. We will look at such a process momentarily.

Planning Process

Second, you need a planning process that can guide in the development of change initiatives that will move the regional body toward the vision. Positive attitudes need to flow into an executable plan. So, you will also need a process for creating such a plan. We will look at a planning process as well.

Conclusion

The first challenge to realizing the vision is preparation. As a leader, you must prepare yourself. You must size the challenge in your particular regional body. And you must make sure you have the proper tools available—both knowledge tools and process tools. We have considered the knowledge tools required already. The next chapter will focus on the process tools.

Engagement Guide

The Purpose

To discuss the three ways to prepare to realize the vision of a robust church development effort.

Personal Reflection on Preparing Yourself.

The chapter noted three personal qualities that a leader needs in order to lead an effort to realize the Robust Vision. A leader must be committed, patient and focused.

- *As you think about yourself as a leader, how committed are you to implementing this vision?*

- *Are you patient? Can you imagine yourself working with people to realize this vision over time? Do you ever recognize in yourself a tendancy toward passivity instead of active engagement?*

- *Are you the kind of person who can keep focused on a goal?*

Group Discussion Questions

Allow for two different parts in your group discussion.

First, ask people who feel free to do so to share some of their personal reflections.

- *What did you hear from each other?*

- *What are the potential implications, both positive and negative from what you heard?*

- *Discuss together the size of the challenge.*

- *What do you think sizing the challenge means in your regional body?*

Finally, discuss the tools necessary to realize the vision. Encourage people to take the *Measure of Robustness* and the *iChange* surveys in preparation for the next Engagement Session following Chapter Seven.

Processes to Realize

This chapter addresses part two of the question: How do you realize the vision of a robust church development effort in your regional body? Three questions were posed:

1. *How do you prepare yourself to realize the vision?*
2. *How do you help people process the need to realize the vision?*
3. *How do you develop a plan for realizing the vision?*

In the previous chapter, the focus was on the first question, preparing to realize. Preparation involves three parts. First is your own preparation as a leader. Second, preparation calls for sizing the magnitude of the challenge in your regional body. Finally, it clarifies the kinds of tools you will need to transform the vision into reality. There were two kinds of tools called for: information tools and process tools. Two kinds of process are called for to respond to questions 2 and 3 above. Question 2 requires a process that facilitates the building of consensus around the need to embrace the Robust Vision. Question 3 points to a process for building a Robust Implementation Plan.

This chapter will provide a process for each of these. Additionally, the Engagement Session is designed to support the implementation of these two processes with your regional body leadership. The chapter will describe and illustrate the processes and the Engagement Session will provide you a guided process.

Building Consensus

We begin by exploring the consensus-building process. The question is this: How do we help people process the need and challenge to realize the vision? Following a case study, a consensus-building process will be outlined that can easily be implemented in your regional body.

Case Study: Families Forward Strategic Planning

I serve on the board of a transitional housing agency called Families Forward (at least I did at the time of writing this). One of my responsibilities is to guide strategic planning. During my first year of service, we needed to develop a new three-year plan. The process began by collecting information from our various constituencies—the board, the clients, donors, granting agencies and our staff. We wanted to know how they felt about the agency and how it operated. We also wanted to get a sense of what they thought about the future of the agency in general and specifically directions for new growth. We currently own and manage 14 homes for families, but we have been promised an additional 14 as a result of a local military base closure in Orange County, California. That would double the capacity of our program. While that sounds great, the operational and fund-raising implications are not trivial.

Because of this, we found a theme embedded in the information suggesting that some members of the board and staff were not as enthusiastic about the possibility of growth as some others. Through the process, we had developed three Strategic Initiatives with strategies and we were well on our way to developing action plans for each when some questions began to emerge. While there was no conflict or animosity, there was a fair level of discomfort and uncertainty about how the agency should respond to growth opportunities.

The Growth Initiative with its strategies are provided as an illustration.

FUTURE GROWTH:

Initiative #3: We will create a proactive framework for determining program extension and service reach that aligns with the Families Forward mission and values.

Strategies

Develop an overall growth philosophy statement that supports our mission and values and considers impacts on existing programs.

Develop criteria for assessing potential new program extension opportunities that includes evaluation of core programs and service effectiveness.

Develop criteria for assessing and modifying extent of service reach.

Apply criteria to Tustin and determine if it should be embraced and what programs should be offered.

The Growth Initiative reflected the need expressed in our collective planning to develop a growth policy that would allow us to assess opportunities as they arose. Initially, we were going to have a small group draft a policy. But it became clear that we did not just need a policy. We needed a process for people to sort through their feelings together and explore the possibilities of growth or no growth. It would be easy enough for a task group to write a policy and to get a large majority of the board to approve it. But we did not need approval. We needed to explore together the sense of fear and uncertainty that surrounded all questions of growth. Financial support of non-profit agencies was dropping across the country. The economy continued to falter. Donors had told us they loved us, but were tapped. And there were several who feared that if we grew larger we would lose the close, personal ethos and approach that had been the hallmark of Families Forward. However, people who serve on such boards and staff do so because they want to help families. The needs were growing. Would we grow to meet the need? Some members were the "climb every mountain type." Others were more conservative, fearing that we would over-extend and lose even what we had.

Before we could state a policy, we needed a process that allowed us to work through these issues together. For people with concerns, to push a growth policy forward would create resentment and negative attitudes. For those who wanted to grow, the same things could occur in the opposite direction. They could begin to resent the conservative folks. In such scenarios—and we have all seen them—conflict, reflected in troublesome attitudes, begins to brew under the surface. If we were to move forward without some consensus-building time, it could hurt the health of the organization. We would very likely see erosion of support. Some board members would make each opportunity a bigger issue than necessary. Others would simply emotionally disengage. Neither scenario is good for the mission.

So, the executive leadership of the agency decided that we needed a process that would bring the 30-plus board and staff members together. The objective of the process was to shape the basic elements of a policy. Yet the more valuable piece of that process was the opportunity for all of us to interact together around our fears and uncertainty, as well as our hopes and dreams for serving people in need.

The kinds of change that the vision for a robust church development effort calls for will, I am sure, create a similar dynamic. In some places it could be minimal, but in others, the potential for conflict or blocking on one side or for reckless pushes for change on the other is very great. Before building a plan, you will need to build consensus and that will take a consensus-building process. Or, as I have referred to it, an attitude-adjustment process that will help reduce fear and uncertainty and increase trust among people.

Steps in Building Consensus

So the first process is a consensus-building process. There are four steps reflected in four questions. We propose you follow just these steps using the resources demonstrated. With some preparation, these steps should be done as an all-day retreat with your leadership.

1. Assess

The first question is this: How closely do we reflect the Vision now? As stated earlier, to embark upon any journey requires you to know two things: where you are and where you want to go. If we assume that the vision of a robust church development effort is where we want to go, then we need to assess where we are. The first step in the process is to understand the current state of your church development effort vis-à-vis the vision. This is of course where the Measure of Robustness tool becomes helpful. Have everyone who will participate in the consensus-building day complete the survey and print a personal report for the retreat.

The first discussion of the day should ask the question: Why are you involved in this work? This question is designed to get people discussing their involvement as an expression of their faith.

The second discussion should revolve around the different results of the Measure of Robustness report. Compare and contrast with the Three Elements of a Robust Vision.

2. Imagine

The next step asks the group to do some collective imagining. Ask the question: What would we look like if the vision were realized in our regional body? If you have a large group, you probably want to break into smaller groups. Each group should record its answers to share them with the whole group. Discuss the themes you find in common.

Once complete, move to the next step.

3. Evaluate

The third step seeks to evaluate the various possible outcomes of either moving, or not moving, toward the realization of the vision. The larger question is this: What are the possible outcomes if we did or did not move to realize the vision? To get at this, you will discuss four questions, one at a time, with sharing in between each step.

This process piece recognizes that there are best possible and worst possible outcomes inherent in either moving forward or maintaining the current status. Follow this sequence.

1. *What are the worst possible outcomes if we move to realize this vision?*

2. *What are the best possible outcomes if we move to realize this vision?*

3. *What are the worst possible outcomes if we do not move to realize this vision?*

4. *What are the best possible outcomes if we do not move to realize this vision?*

4. Commit

The last step of this process is the question: Will we commit ourselves to realizing the vision? Based upon an evaluation of the best and worst possible outcomes of realizing or not, what do we want to do? To what will we commit ourselves?

If the process has been well facilitated, people should feel they have been heard and their concerns addressed at some level. Not everyone will necessarily be fully on board, but everyone should feel that they have been granted a voice and as a result, trust levels will have been raised. The question then becomes: Will you go forward? What is required to feel confident that forward movement is justified? The group must determine what level of consensus is required. According to Marylyn Tabor of Organizational Dynamics, "Very few decisions require 100% consensus. Nearly all decisions can be implemented if a sufficient number of people (70% or more, depending upon the issue) agree to support the decision or at least refrain from sabotaging it."

Note: You may want to engage the services of a skilled facilitator to guide this process. Percept can make recommendations.

Return to Families Forward Story—What Happened?

So, what happened with Families Forward? We conducted the consensus-building workshop pretty much as outlined above. By the end of the day, we had given voice to our hopes and fears and through that created the basic ideas of a growth policy.

> *"Helping families help themselves" is at the core of Families Forward's mission and values. While we recognize that there are limitations to the extent of service reach and programs that can be offered, we nonetheless believe that helping families must always be our primary concern. Insofar as families will continue to need such assistance, Families Forward will continue to consider new ways and opportunities to provide assistance. We recognize that this statement implies a willingness to let the agency's reach extend and its programs broaden.*
>
> *However, this willingness must be governed by prudence. Therefore the Families Forward Board will consider new opportunity proposals as long as such proposals:*
>
> - *Complement our core mission*
>
> - *Correspond to our philosophy of service delivery*
>
> - *Sustain the quality of existing services without compromise*
>
> - *Demonstrate the financial support necessary to grow without jeopardizing existing programs*
>
> - *Support the infrastructure necessary to carry the additional load*

The policy creates a pair of brackets. On one side, we embraced the need to grow to meet growing needs. That is part of our mission. But on the other, we said the growth opportunity must meet certain criteria. If a growth opportunity would cause us to violate any of these, it would not be embraced. The board and staff were happy. There was consensus. Now we could continue our planning process. This takes us as well to the second process.

Building a Robust Plan

Assuming through the consensus-building process that you have strong enough agreement to move forward, your next step is to develop a plan that will help you realize the vision. The question now is this: What must we do in what order and within what timeframe to realize the vision? In other words, what is the plan for implementing the robust vision?

This process should be done separately and following the consensus-building process. But you will capitalize on the momentum the consensus-building process created. Only the main steps of the process are outlined. Essentially, it represents the five steps for developing a plan of action.

1. Clarify

Begin by revisiting the results of the assessment. Ask yourselves: What are our current strengths and weaknesses based upon the Assessment? Using the results of the Assessment, determine where you are strong and weak. Build lists of both and discuss the reasons you believe you are weak and or strong on any particular item from the Assessment Report.

2. List

The next step is to develop a list of things that need to change if you are to realize the vision. Ask yourselves: What do we need to do to begin to realize the vision in its particulars? Restate the list in the form of Change Initiative statements. I like these to begin in this manner, "We will...."

3. Prioritize

The list must now be prioritized. How should these Change Initiatives be prioritized? Put the list of Change Initiatives in priority order based upon what is of greatest importance and which you are most likely to successfully implement. When reflecting, keep these two principles in mind. First, build on strengths while isolating and minimizing, where possible, weaknesses. Strength begets strength. Too much focus on weakness demoralizes. Certainly weaknesses must be dealt with, but building on your strengths provides the necessary energy to face the weaknesses.

But also consider this second principle. Some Practices are more important in sequence than others. For example, if you are really weak on leadership-related practices, perhaps work on these first. This will build capacity for dealing with others.

When this step is complete, you will have a set of Change Initiatives. The assumption is that if you were to accomplish what these initiatives outline, you would move closer to the realization of the vision.

4. Strategize

The Change Initiatives focus your attention where change needs to occur. But there are many ways to implement the initiatives. The next step is to strategize together and then write strategies that if enacted would result in the implementation of the Initiatives. Each initiative will have more than one strategy.

The question for this step is this: What strategies should we pursue to accomplish the Change Initiatives?

Take each initiative one at a time. Brainstorm the different ways each initiative could be accomplished. Extract from the brainstormed items through elimination or consolidation those strategies that would enable you to carry out the Change Initiative. It is best if these begin with an action verb.

5. Action Plan

The final step in building your plan is called the Action Plan. The action plan addresses nitty-gritty details such as what, when, who, in what order and how much. The step asks: What action steps do we need to take, in what order and within what timeframe? The components of an Action Plan are:

1. *What needs to be done?*
2. *When do we need to start?*
3. *When should this task be finished?*
4. *Who is the primary person responsible?*
5. *What resources (financial, time, etc) will be needed?*

When these five steps are complete, you will have a plan for realizing the vision in your regional body. The next step is to implement your plan. Note, this is not a strategic plan for church development. Indeed, if you do not have one, your Change plan may indicate that this is a task to complete. The focus of this plan is on moving your regional body toward closer alignment with the three elements of a robust church development effort. Think of it as a macro framework for change. Its focus is on how you function more than what you do in conducting church development.

Conclusion

The difference between a dream that is wishful thinking and one that is a captivating vision is certainly in the power of the vision and a leader's commitment to its becoming real. But right after that, a good leader realizes that she or he needs a game plan for realizing that vision. This task has been the focus of this chapter. It has been very practical; most conversations that deal with the "how" questions are. They generally are not the really elegant discussions, but they are essential if ideas are to be turned into reality. So, to realize the vision of a robust church development effort, you must first prepare yourself and make sure you have the necessary knowledge and process tools available to you. Second, you need to build consensus for the vision and the need to see your regional body transformed toward that vision. Finally, you need to build the plan to realize the vision.

Engagement Guide

The Purposes

- *To build consensus for implementing the Robust Vision.*

- *To build a plan for implementation of the Robust Vision.*

Background Information and Recommendations

This Engagement Guide, unlike the others, assumes more than one session together. Thus it is divided into two parts. Part I will guide your leadership in the consensus-building process around the implementation of the Robust Vision. Part II will guide in the development of a plan for implementation of the Robust Vision.

We would recommend that each part be done as a single session, separate from the other. Each session can probably be done in about four hours. But it is not recommended that you attempt to do both in a single day. Consensus building is such that time is needed after the process is complete to allow the experience to settle into people's hearts and minds. However we do not recommend that much time pass between the two processes.

Unlike the prior Engagement Discussions, you will want to keep careful records of all discussions.

Group Discussion Questions

Part I: Building Consensus

1. Assess

The first step is to complete the Assessment tool, A Measure of Robustness. To do so, you must be a Percept client. If you are, log on to your VISTA2000 site and complete the survey. If you are reading this book as a group, have everyone complete the survey, print the results and bring them to your consensus-building day session.

- *What is the general Measure of Robustness of your Regional Body?*

- *Do the results of the various persons who took the survey generally agree or do they disagree considerably? Discuss why, ether way.*

- *Where are you weak? Where are you strong?*

2. Imagine

What would church development look like if this vision were realized in our various traditions? Brainstorm together, posting your thoughts on newsprint.

3. Evaluate

This step seeks to evaluate the various possible outcomes of either moving forward, or not, toward the realization of the vision. What are the possible outcomes if we did or did not move to realize the vision in our denominational traditions across the country? To address this question, we have broken it into four smaller questions. Work through each question separately.

- *What are the worst possible outcomes if we move to realize this vision?*

- *What are the best possible outcomes if we move to realize this vision?*

- *What are the worst possible outcomes if we do not move to realize this vision?*

- *What are the best possible outcomes if we do not move to realize this vision?*

4. Commit

Having considered the implications of implementing this vision from four different angles, you are ready to discuss the next question. It has to do with making a commitment.

Will you commit yourselves to implementing this vision?

Allow each person an opportunity to reflect on this question and share with the total group. When everyone has shared, discuss what appears to be the group's consensus about the question.

Part II: Outlining a Plan

If you decided that you did want to commit yourselves to implementing this vision, then you need a plan for doing so. This process will assist you in the development of a plan.

1. Clarify

Review again the lists of strengths and weaknesses relative to the Measure of Robustness. Have the lists available from the consensus-building process.

- *Again, where are you weak?*

- *Where are you strong?*

- *Where would be the best place to begin, based upon the two principles outlined in the chapter?*

2. List

Build a list of what needs to change if you are to realize the Robust Vision in your regional body. Consolidate ideas where possible so that your list is clean and without redundancies. Try to reduce the list to no more than five items.

Transform the list into a set of statements of intent. "We will...."

3. Prioritize

Prioritize your list. It may prove helpful to have each person create a priority list. Each item on the list is given a score from 1 to "N." Tabulate how each member of the group scored an item. A simple method of prioritization is to simply add up the scores. The highest priority items will have the lowest scores. Once you have the list, then discuss it to make sure everyone is in fact comfortable with the prioritization scheme. Negotiate if necessary.

4. Strategize

Take each Initiative and brainstorm possible ways—strategies—by which you might complete an Initiative.

5. Action Plan

Develop an action plan for each strategy. It may not be necessary or possible to do this step as part of the planning session. It may be enough to outline the strategies and then assign persons to complete the action plan step.

The action plan addresses nitty-gritty details such as what, when, who, in what order and how much. The components of an Action Plan are:

1. *What needs to be done?*

2. *When do we need to start?*

3. *When should this task be finished?*

4. *Who is the primary person responsible?*

5. *What resources (financial, time, etc.) will be needed?*

8

Embracing the Dream

In this brief book we have reflected on a vision for robust church development efforts for regional level denominational bodies. A particular shape to that vision has been proposed. It is comprised of three elements: a passionate faith, efforts founded upon missiological principles and agencies structured around the 10 Best Practices. We have considered how to realize that vision in our regional bodies in some very practical ways. (And if you have completed the Engagement Guide activities, you even have a rough draft of an implementation plan.) Now it is time to shift the focus to the work ahead.

In this closing chapter, I want to return to the first question of a robust effort. Why do you bother? Not all of what has been outlined is easy to swallow. The reality is, based upon an analysis of the 10 Best Practices many regional bodies are struggling. Yours may be one of them. So, why do you bother? What makes you get out of bed every day and engage the task? Do you ever allow yourself to ask this question?

The first element of our vision is a passionate faith. While I believe the missiological principles are critical and the 10 Best Practices are foundational to a robust effort, it is this first element that will make the difference. Without it, the other two elements are empty shells. For the dream of a robust effort to be more than wishful thinking, for it to be a captivating vision, we must embrace that vision. And embracing the vision is all about a passionate faith. So in this last chapter, I want us to reflect again on this element of the vision. I believe it is critical to embracing the overall vision and it is a good place to finish the book and hopefully launch your effort.

Embrace

Let's first consider what I mean by embracing the vision. Embrace is a word picture. Imagine a person reaching out with both arms and pulling something in close. I embrace what I cherish or what I perceive to be of great value. To embrace an idea means to take ownership of it, to make it yours. To embrace an idea is more than understanding it intellectually. It is to move from the position of outside, looking in on it, to the action of stepping into it. To embrace the vision is to make it your vision. There are two points I would like to make about this notion of embrace.

Two Ways of Knowing the Vision

Some years ago, I read a brief essay by C. S. Lewis titled "Meditation in a Toolshed." He was reflecting on two ways of knowing. Let me share a brief excerpt:

> I was standing today in the dark toolshed. The sun was shining outside and through the crack at the top of the door there came a sunbeam. From where I stood that beam of light, with the specks of dust floating in it, was the most striking thing in the place. Everything else was almost pitch black. I was seeing the beam, not seeing things by it.

> Then I moved, so that the beam fell on my eyes. Instantly the whole previous picture vanished. I saw no tool shed, and (above all) no beam. Instead I saw, framed in the irregular cranny at the top of the door, green leaves moving on the branches of a tree outside and beyond, ninety-odd million miles away, the sun. Looking along the beam, and looking at the beam are very different experiences.

What moved me at the time about this essay was the fact that my approach to faith tended toward the intellectual. I shied away from the experiential. It has always been easier for me to talk about the faith than allow myself to experience the faith. I felt one was more real than the other. Lewis, no intellectual lightweight, felt that intellectual analysis was only one way of seeing something. It was valid, but inadequate if exclusive. Through his essay, he points out that in stepping into the beam of light, he stopped looking at the beam, in fact it became invisible. But by looking along it, he could see new wonders and beauty—rather, he could experience them because he became a participant in the beam and not just an observer of the beam.

When I talk about embracing the vision, I am talking about stepping into the beam. We can talk about church development all day long. But until we step into the beam, we have not really embraced it. We have been talking about it and the information is critical. The vision that has been outlined is significant. But we must do more than talk about it if we would see it realized. We must embrace it. We must step into it. We must give ourselves to the vision.

Two Ways of Embracing

The second point I would like to make about the idea of embrace is that it can be viewed from two perspectives. There is the perspective of the one doing the embracing. But there is also the perspective of the one being embraced. If to embrace means to take into one's self and to make it your own, to be embraced means it takes you and makes you its own. To answer the question, why do you bother, we must see ourselves as both embraced and embracing, and in that order. I believe a captivating vision embraces us before we embrace the vision. To embrace a vision is to be first embraced by the vision.

Is this not what happens to Abraham and Sarah? Hear Genesis 12:1-8:

> Now the LORD said to Abram, "Go from your country and your kindred and your father's house to the land that I will show you. I will make of you a great nation, and I will bless you, and make your name great, so that you will be a blessing. I will bless those who bless you, and the one who curses you I will curse; and in you all the families of the earth shall be blessed."

> So Abram went, as the LORD had told him; and Lot went with him. Abram was seventy-five years old when he departed from Haran. Abram took his wife Sarai and his brother's son Lot, and all the possessions that they had gathered, and the persons whom they had acquired in Haran; and they set forth to go to the land of Canaan. When they had come to the land of Canaan,

> Abram passed through the land to the place at Shechem, to the oak of Moreh. At that time the Canaanites were in the land. Then the LORD appeared to Abram, and said, "To your offspring I will give this land." So he built there an altar to the LORD, who had appeared to him. From there he moved on to the hill country on the east of Bethel, and pitched his tent, with Bethel on the west

and Ai on the east; and there he built an altar to the LORD and invoked the name of the LORD.

Encounters between God and humans always begin with God in the biblical story. Within the flow of the book of Genesis, the story of Abraham and Sarah and their family is important to the Israelites' self-identity. Put into its final form perhaps somewhere between the tenth and ninth centuries B.C., Genesis explains who the people of Israel were and why they existed as a people. Their identity was rooted in a promise given to these two ancient individuals. And that promise is directly tied to the prior 11 chapters of Genesis. It is proposed as a direct solution to the problem of disobedience and violence that was introduced into the world in chapter 3 when the first humans turned to darkness. Humans were created to enjoy intimate relationship with God but through disobedience, had been separated and in their separation, were inclined to do all manner of violence toward each other and God's creation. To this day, we still are inclined to follow the way of Cain.

God, however, intends to solve this problem and redeem his creation. And how will this be done? Through a special family that Genesis traces back to the alternative line of Seth, God calls out a family living in Ur of the Chaldeans. To the patriarch and matriarch of this family, Abram and Sarai, he makes a promise. Their descendants would be given a land. Their descendants would be as numerous as the sand in the sea or the stars of heaven. And through their descendants, all other peoples would be blessed. This is a magnificent vision, and Genesis repeats it in one form or another four times in the Abraham and Sarah story cycle.

Now let's use some creative imagination and transport ourselves back in time to the moment Abram first received the call. We know he responded to God's call and left Haran. We know all of the different twists and turns the story took before Isaac is born and afterwards. But what if Abram had not responded to God's call? What if he had only looked at the promise but not stepped into the promise? Presumably, we would have a different story—maybe a different family through whom the blessing would come to the rest of us. But Abraham and Sarah did respond. God's vision for them and their posterity embraced them first and in faith, they stepped into the vision and embraced it in turn. The vision presented by God first embraced them—it captured them, took ownership of them. And in response, they embraced and acted and the rest is part of our history.

This is the order for us as well. We must first be embraced by God's vision before we can embrace the vision. God set before Abraham and Sarah a captivating vision. It embraced them. And in response, they embraced the vision. They took it to heart. They made it theirs and in so doing, they stepped forth in faith. Having been embraced, they in passionate faith embraced the vision. To put it another way, passionate faith is a response to the faithfulness of God.

And if we consider Lewis' two ways of knowing, being embraced and responding by embracing is to step into the beam and not just look at the beam. Remember that once he stepped into the beam, he was no longer aware of the beam, he had become part of the beam and he was only aware of what he could experience within the beam. It embraced him, he embraced it and wonderful new worlds opened to him. If we are not willing to step into the vision, we will accomplish little more than to talk about the vision. Such talk is merely wishful thinking.

The Embracing Vision

Let's shift our focus for a moment to the vision. I really doubt that the vision for a robust church development effort outlined in this book is of such a quality as to have this kind of embracing capacity. That is not to say I am backing away from it. Rather, what I want to do is connect it to the larger vision of what God is doing, to effectively connect it back to the promise to Abraham and Sarah and right up to our understanding of the church and its mission in our culture.

Story of My Vision for the Church

Let me share a personal story with you. Some years ago, I was filling out an application for additional graduate studies. I was asked to tell my faith story and relate it to my call to service in the church. Here is what I wrote:

> I grew up in Corvallis, Oregon. My spiritual journey (at least that I am aware of) began on a January evening in 1970 when I was a senior in high school. Active involvement in a church was not part of my upbringing. Rather, I was introduced to Jesus during the beginning of the youth revivals (also known as the Jesus movement) of the early 70s. Initially, the only churches in Oregon open to us "hippie types" were Pentecostal, so I quickly found myself involved in one. Upon graduation from high school, I moved to the Seattle area and eventually graduated from Seattle Pacific College. During my college years, I participated in several youth related ministries, including two coffeehouses. Later, my wife and I worked

in ministries with post-collegiate singles. Ultimately I ended up in the Presbyterian Church where I was ordained.

It was during those formative years that two things occurred. First, I realized that the idea of the church was very powerful and attractive to me. Perhaps because I am an idealistic boomer, I found in the notion of the people of God something that seemed so right, so promising and so magnificent. Second, I realized that the church was very far from that ideal image. Such realizations are a serious blow to idealists and of course I was not the only one of my generation drawing these conclusions. But many of my friends opted out of the church either by going off to do their own thing or by becoming involved in one of the many para-church ministries. With a few of my close friends, however, I chose to stay in the church and to do ministry from within. I believed even then that the local church as a visible expression of the community of faith was the center of God's mission and so that is where I wanted to anchor my life and ministry.

And that has been the theme of my entire adult life. From very early in my own pilgrimage, my desire has been to see the church be what God intends it to be, in some form. For I believe it is through the church that God is telling his story and seeing that story change lives. That is the story that makes the idea of the church so wonderfully compelling. And because of this, I long to see the church effectively engage North American culture with the message and ministry of the Gospel. I dream of thousands of healthy, vibrant churches actively engaging in ministry in and among their communities of residence. It is this particular vision that has been and continues to be the driving force of my life and ministry.

This is what I wrote. This is what I still believe. And this is why I bother. This vision is so captivating that I am compelled to step into its beam. It is an embracing vision.

Church development as Embracing Vision

I suspect that you could tell a similar story. But how do we get to this marvelous vision for church development in general and specifically, the vision articulated for a robust effort? I would contend that this specific vision for church development is derived directly from the larger vision of Christ's church in the world. This may be obvious to you, but let's consider it anyway. Why do we do church development? Because we want to see healthy, vital and effective congregations that exist in communities as a sign, a foretaste, an agency of and a witness to the redemptive reign of God. I suspect many of us have had glimpses of this alternative reality. Or perhaps you have had small experiences where you have encountered this alternative reality and it felt good. And, we want to see it replicated, do we not? Is this not, yet again, a vision we find compelling? Or, to put it another way, an embracing vision? Church development efforts are simply a vehicle for seeing this replication occur in many different places. As such, church development is an embracing vision. The vision of vital congregations existing as islands of hope, faith and love is embracing. I want to experience it! I want to see others experience it. So, the vision of such congregations embraces me. I am pulled toward it. I am pulled into it.

Embracing the Vision

God has set before us an embracing vision. The question for us is, will we embrace it? Beautiful as the vision is, and embracing as it is, you and I must still embrace it. We must step into it and not just look at it. This question brings us back to the first element of our robust vision for church development, a passionate faith. Being embraced by God is the root of a passionate faith. And it is a passionate faith that is necessary in turn to embrace the vision of a robust church development effort.

The Power of Passionate Faith

But what does a passionate faith look like? Let me share two more stories with you. They not only give meaning to the idea of a passionate faith they also demonstrate its power. Both stories are very personal, but powerful.

Mom's Story

The year I celebrated my fiftieth birthday, my mother and father came down to California from Oregon. Now you must understand, this was a somewhat unusual occurrence. My immediate family has lived in Southern California since 1980 and in that period, my parents had made it down maybe six or seven times. In the late 1990s I began to notice new life in my mother, life that I had not seen even while growing up. Some years earlier she had become very involved in her Methodist church. I was glad because I felt it gave her a supportive community. But to be perfectly honest, I never thought of it beyond the purely human aspect.

While visiting, she mentioned that she had given a talk to the United Methodist Women on her faith journey. Now to my credit, I kept my composure but inside I was thinking, You have got to be kidding, my mother sharing about her faith journey before a group? Unheard of! I asked if I could read what she wrote, and she sent it to me. I was captivated. Here is how she began her comments:

> "My first introduction to God came at a small German Baptist Sunday School where I grew up in Stafford (Oregon). Once a year, I go back there to the little white Church for what some of you have heard me call my 'cemetery day.' This is sacred ground for me. This is where I first truly met God."

It also, she tells me, is where she and Dad want to be buried, a little pioneer graveyard in the Oregon countryside. The story continues as she tells how she met my dad at the very Methodist Church she now attends. But married life and children caused her to drift, she explained:

> "As the years passed, I felt myself becoming more and more disconnected. It seemed as if my vision of God was becoming fogged. I felt as if I was losing my closeness all together. As I look back now, I may have misplaced God, but I was not misplaced."

She concludes with this:

> "I don't know where I will go from here, but I know who will be in charge."

This is an expression of passionate faith. I wanted to cry upon reading it. But I did not know how. I was just stunned and deeply moved!

Jonathan's Story

My eldest son, Jonathan, is a Ph.D. student at the University of Colorado at Boulder. He chose Boulder for its program but equally because there are lots of large mountains within 30 minutes of the school. He climbs mountains, scales rocks and loves ice climbing. During his 2002 Christmas break, he and some friends traveled to an area called Ouray in southwestern Colorado where there is an ice-climbing park. He called home to tell us he had returned safely to Boulder, but he also told me that he would send me an email the next day telling a story about his experience. After receiving the email, I understood why he wanted to write it instead of just tell me. Written correspondence allows you to avoid hearing things from your father such as, "Oh my God!"

The worst nightmare for my wife and me is that something will happen on one of Jonathan's climbs. Well, it had happened. A friend from California had come out to climb with him. Though it was getting late in the day, there was one more ice face his friend really wanted to scale. Jonathan did not think it was a good idea, but did not want to disappoint his friend. They climbed the 1000-foot face, but when they got to the top, a snowstorm hit. Hear his own words:

> *Once we got to the top, a snowstorm had come in and we couldn't see much of anything. It was total white out up there and what we could see of our descent route looked very dangerous and scary. So we kept moving sideways along the mountain trying to find a safe way to get down, but we couldn't. I was scared to death at this point and I started remembering all the horror stories that started off just like ours, where the people got caught on the mountain, got frost bite, lost toes, fingers and their noses or just died. I was determined to get down though. We eventually realized that we didn't have enough time to get down and we should find a place to hide out for the night. We searched all over the place, but the mountain slope averaged at an angle of about 50 degrees and there was nowhere to make a snow shelter. So with about 15 minutes of light left we ended up at a tree about 1000 feet off the ground. We made a bench out of snow to sit on and we put on every bit of warm clothing we had.*

He explains that they tied themselves to the tree to keep from sliding down the mountain and hunkered down for the night. He continues:

> *I was really scared at this point and I started thinking about my family and friends and how there was so much at Flatirons (that is his church) that I still wanted to do. We thought that this was*

the first night of a 3-day storm and we didn't know if we were going to make it or not. Suddenly I realized the situation I was in, in context with my relationship with the Lord. I remembered that most of my best experiences with God were in really bad situations like this, only not quite this bad. Then I saw this as an experience with God, a time to see him do his work.

This is passionate faith as well. Passionate faith sees life through the lens of one's relationship to God. And that lens results in a different interpretation of an event or life process and different expectation of an outcome even if, in my son's case, that outcome might have been his own demise. Abraham and Sarah's response to God's vision was similar. The promise to Abraham is laid out again in Genesis 15.

He [the LORD] brought him outside and said, "Look toward heaven and count the stars, if you are able to count them." Then he said to him, "So shall your descendants be" (v. 5).

Abram's response to this vision was faith.

And he believed the LORD; and the LORD reckoned it to him as righteousness (v. 6).

Passionate Faith Is the Vehicle for Embracing the Vision

Passionate faith is the human response to the vision of God. It begins with God's vision for redeeming creation. It extends through the unfolding story of God realizing God's vision for redemption, and it anchors in our own encounter with God's vision for our own life. From there, it turns outward again and connects God's vision for our life with the unfolding vision of redemption as it proceeds into the future until that eschatological moment when redemption is complete. My mother, after a many-year hiatus, found herself again embraced by God's vision and once back in the beam, realized she had never been abandoned. My son, clinging to that mountainside, connected his life experiences with the saving hand of God and connected that with his own sense of calling into the future. For me, seeing this in both my mother and my son connected my life with the larger, unfolding vision being realized in some manner across three generations of Regeles.

Passionate faith is our response to God's story and results in our stepping into the beam and taking our place in that unfolding story. As such, it is the vehicle for embracing that vision that embraces us. For Dr. Martin

Luther King, Jr., the dream of freedom and liberty for all Americans was a captivating vision that was connected to God's larger redemptive vision. He was so captivated by that vision that he embraced it with passionate faith. And that faith empowered a commitment to realize the vision. It was not just wishful thinking. It was a captivating vision that he worked to realize through action.

More Than Just Wishful Thinking

Hopefully our vision of a robust church development effort is more than just wishful thinking. Hopefully it is of the same order as Dr. King's—a captivating and compelling vision that a passionate faith drives us to embrace. You are the key to realizing this vision in your regional body. You must personally embrace it as critical to the future effectiveness of your regional body and its congregations. It must be a particular expression of your faith. If you cannot imagine it and be so captivated by the vision that you will work to realize it, it is not likely to happen.

Let me conclude with some questions. Are you willing to let this vision of a robust church development vision embrace you? Are you willing to embrace it? Are you willing to step into it or will you stand outside its beam and only talk about it? We can talk about church development all day long. But until we step into the beam, we have not really embraced it. The vision that has been outlined is significant. But we must do more than talk about it if we would see it realized. We must embrace it. We must step into it. We must, as an expression of our faith, give ourselves to the vision if we would see it realized. Are you willing to embrace the vision by making a commitment now to initiate a process of realizing the vision as it has been shaped in the preceding pages?

Conclusion

Let me return now to my initial question to you, why do you bother? I believe you bother, like me, because God has given you a glimpse of the vision that his grace is unfolding in our world, and its wonder and beauty is compelling. We want to step into the light and become lost in it. Our hearts sense that in that wonder is hope for us, for our loved ones and for our world. This vision captures us and in faith, we embrace it. Embrace this vision for your church development efforts as one more extension of that which has embraced you.

The Lord, the Creator of heaven and earth,
bless and guide you in all that you do,
confirm and strengthen you in all goodness,
and keep you in life which is eternal.[1]
Amen

Engagement Guide

The Purpose

To challenge one another to embrace the vision and commit to its implementation in your regional body.

Group Discussion Questions

Discuss these questions with those who have studied this book with you. Some of them may be difficult. Some may be a bit uncomfortably direct. They all call upon you to root your responses in your faith.

- *Do you find the Robust Vision outlined in this book for a regional body church development effort compelling?*

- *This final chapter states that "You are the key to realizing this vision in your regional body." How do you respond to this statement, both emotionally and intellectually?*

- *Do you feel you have the passion of faith to provide leadership in the implementation of this vision?*

- *Are you ready and willing to let it embrace you and in turn embrace it? Are you willing to commit to more than talking about the vision? Are you willing to commit to implementing the vision?*

ENDNOTES

[1] David Adam, The Rhythm of Life: Celtic Daily Prayer (Harrisburg, PA: Morehouse Publishing, 1996), p. 33.

Other Percept Resources...

*For more information
about Percept Resources go to
www.Percept.info*

Percept 29889 Santa Margarita Pkwy, Rancho Santa Margarita, CA 92688-3609
949.635.1282 Phone   949.635.1283 Fax   800.442.6277 Toll Free
www.Percept.info (web address)   info@perceptnet.com (e-mail)